MARITIME HISTORY SERIES

Series Editor

John B. Hattendorf, *Naval War College*

Volumes Published in this Series

Pietro Martire d'Anghiera, et al.
The history of travayle in the West and East Indies (1577)
Introduction by Thomas R. Adams,
John Carter Brown Library

Alvise Cà da Mosto
Questa e una opera necessaria a tutti li naviga[n]ti (1490)
bound with:
Pietro Martire d'Anghiera
Libretto de tutta la navigatione de Re de Spagna (1504)
Introduction by Felipe Fernández-Armesto,
Oxford University

Martín Cortés
The arte of navigation (1561)
Introduction by D. W. Waters,
National Maritime Museum, Greenwich

John Davis
The seamans secrets (1633)
Introduction by A. N. Ryan, University of Liverpool

Francisco Faleiro
Tratado del esphera y del arte del marear (1535)
Introduction by Onesimo Almeida, Brown University

Gemma, Frisius
De principiis astronomiae & cosmographiae (1553)
Introduction by C. A. Davids, University of Leiden

Tobias Gentleman
Englands way to win wealth, and to employ ships and marriners
(1614)
bound with:
Robert Kayll
The trades increase (1615)
and
Dudley Digges
The defence of trade (1615)
and
Edward Sharpe
Britaines busse (1615)
Introduction by John B. Hattendorf, Naval War College

Pedro de Medina
L'art de naviguer (1554)
Introduction by Carla Rahn Phillips, University of Minnesota

Jean Taisnier
A very necessarie and profitable booke concerning navigation (1585?)
Introduction by Uwe Schnall,
Deutsches Schiffahrtsmuseum, Bremerhaven

Lodovico de Varthema
Die ritterlich un[d] lobwirdig Rayss (1515)
Introduction by George Winius, University of Leiden

Gerrit de Veer
The true and perfect description of three voyages (1609)
Introduction by Stuart M. Frank, Kendall Whaling Museum

Englands way to win wealth, and to employ ships and marriners

(1614)

Tobias Gentleman

together with

Robert Kayll, *The trades increase* **(1615)**
Dudley Digges, *The defence of trade* **(1615)**
Edward Sharpe, *Britaines busse* **(1615)**

Facsimile Reproductions
With an Introduction by

JOHN B. HATTENDORF

Published for the
JOHN CARTER BROWN LIBRARY
by
SCHOLARS' FACSIMILES & REPRINTS
DELMAR. NEW YORK
1992

SCHOLARS' FACSIMILES & REPRINTS
ISSN 0161-7729
SERIES ESTABLISHED 1936
VOLUME 476

New matter in this edition
© 1992 Academic Resources Corporation
All rights reserved

Printed and made in the United States of America

The publication of this work was assisted by a grant from the
National Endowment for the Humanities,
an agency of the Federal government

Reproduced from a copy in,
and with the permission of,
the John Carter Brown Library
at Brown University

Library of Congress Cataloging-in-Publication Data

Gentleman, Tobias.
England's way to win wealth, and to employ ships and marriners (1614) / Tobias Gentleman ; facsimile reproductions with an introduction by John B. Hattendorf
  p.   cm. —
(Scholars' Facsimiles & Reprints, ISSN 0161-7729 ; v. 476)
(Maritime history series)
Reprint. Originally published: London : Nathaniel Butter, 1614.
Includes bibliographical references.
Contents: The trades increase (1615) / Robert Kayll — The defence of trade (1615) / Dudley Digges — Britaines busse (1615) / Edward Sharpe.
ISBN 0-8201-1476-6
1. Great Britain—Commerce—History—17th century. 2. Great Britain—Commercial policy. 3. Herring industry—Great Britain—History—17th century. 4. East India Company. I. Kayll, Robert. Trades increase (1615). 1992. II. Digges, Dudley, Sir, 1583-1639. Defence of trade (1615). 1992. III. E. S. (Edward Sharpe), 17th cent. Britaines busse (1615). 1992. IV. John Carter Brown Library. V. Title. VI. Title: Trades increase (1615) VII. Title: Defence of trade (1615) VIII. Title: Britaines busse (1615) IX. Series: Maritime history series (Delmar, N.Y.)
HF3504.4G46   1992
382'.0942—dc20   92-21728
CIP

Introduction

Pamphlets, by their very nature, are suspect sources. Written for political purposes, they usually represent only one side of an issue, perhaps even bending the facts to fit their views. However, when one uses pamphlets with care and a full understanding of their context, they can be very useful, provide information not easily available elsewhere, and highlight opinions and issues.

In English economic history, the early seventeenth century was a period of chartered companies, trading monopolies, and aggressive commercial protection. Many disputes that arose at this time had their origins in issues connected with trading and fishing privileges. The four pamphlets reproduced in this volume from the collection of the John Carter Brown Library, *England's Way to Win Wealth, The Trade's Increase, The Defence of Trade,* and *Britaine's Busse,* were all published consecutively within a few months of each other in 1614-1615, one reacting to the other. Appearing in the middle of the reign of King James I, the pamphlets came at a brief moment of stagnation in the English shipping industry, during an era that was generally one of maritime expansion in both trade and fishing.[1]

Fishing for herring is one of the oldest continuing maritime activities in Northern Europe. Beginning in the twelfth and thirteenth centuries, the first great fishing ground for herring was in the Baltic off southern Sweden, but by the sixteenth century, that fishery had declined as the fish

INTRODUCTION

migrated away from the Baltic to the North Sea coasts of Norway and Britain. In the fifteenth century, herring fishermen had already begun to search elsewhere for their catch, changing from a coastal to a deep-sea fishery. This brought changes in the shipbuilding industry, requiring the construction of a decked vessel carrying a larger crew. First built in Holland about 1416, this 75-foot-long fishing boat of 70 to 100 tons, specially designed for this fishery became known as a buss.

In this period, the Dutch developed also a successful method of salting the herring, allowing them to carry the fish from distant fishing grounds as well as to use them as commodities for trade from the Baltic to Portugal and Spain. Thus, salt and herring became key elements of the Dutch carrying trade and important elements in Dutch economic development.

In this context, one major general issue of the period was the growth of economic rivalry between the Dutch and the English. Following the assassination of William the Silent in 1584 and Parma's capture of Antwerp, Elizabeth I had openly supported the rebellion of the Dutch provinces against Spain, taking the towns of Flushing and Brill, with the fort of Rammekens, as a pledge for repayment of England's loans and costs. Dutch and English forces complemented one another on land and at sea. The Dutch blockaded the ports that held the transports for carrying troops for the invasion of England in 1588, leaving the Armada unable to carry out Spain's long planned attack. An English brigade joined the forces of Maurice of Nassau, and an Englishman sat on the Council of State. As the Dutch Republic grew and became less dependent on English assistance, friction developed, but there were also strong communities of interest that helped to

INTRODUCTION

promote friendly cooperation.

When James I came to the throne in 1603, his chief aim in foreign policy was to be on friendly terms with Spain and, in the following year, he concluded a peace with Spain and the archdukes in the Low Counties. Exhausted by the long war, Spain finally came to terms with the Dutch, signing a truce in April 1609 that dealt with the Dutch on their terms, treating them as an independent state and secretly conceding to them trade rights in the Indies.

As those negotiations were drawing to a close in early 1609, the Dutch jurist, Huig van Groot, better known as Hugo Grotius, published his *Mare Liberum*. Designed to be the twelfth chapter of his study "De Jure Prædæ" that Grotius wrote as a counsel for the Dutch East India Company, it was part of an argument against Portugal's claim to exclusive rights of navigation in the East Indies under the division of colonial possessions between Spain and Portugal in Pope Alexander VI's bull *Inter Cætera* and the Treaty of Tordesillas in 1494. In this context, Grotius argued that the seas were open to all by Natural Law, and no state could appropriate them. Appearing separately from the main work, the English took Grotius's statement not, as he had intended, in general terms applying to the Portuguese claim. The English thought Grotius was criticizing their long-held views on British sovereignty of the Narrow Seas and because of this they raised an entirely different issue on fishing rights in circumscribed coastal waters. Thus began a long and bitter controversy in which the first rebuttal on the English side was William Wellwood's pamphlet, *Abridgement of all the Sea Laws* in 1613, followed nearly twenty years later by John Selden's famous *Mare Clausum*.

On 16 May 1609, James I issued a proclamation that

INTRODUCTION

immediately strained Anglo-Dutch relations. It followed the publication of Grotius's work by only two or three months and came just five weeks after signing the peace treaty. While many Dutchmen had been suspicious of James I's motives during the peace negotiations, few suspected that he would strike so soon at one of the most important Dutch industries. The king's proclamation declared that "no person of what Nation or qualitie soeuer . . . be permitted to fish vpon any of our Coasts and Seas of Great Britain, Ireland and the rest of the Isles adjacent, . . . untill they haue orderly demanded and obtained Licenses from vs."[2]

The proclamation started a series of Anglo-Dutch diplomatic negotiations over fishing rights. The first Dutch mission to discuss the issue reached England in 1610 and succeeded in persuading James to postpone putting the proclamation into execution for two years. The key factor in this decision was James I's need to maintain good relations with the Dutch. The specific issue at this early stage leading up to the Thirty Years War was the disputed settlement of the succession in Jülich-Cleves, a duchy which lay astride the Rhine along the eastern border of the Dutch Republic.

James's postponement in executing the 1609 proclamation remained in effect until 1616. Although deeper considerations in foreign relations prevented a change in English policy toward the Dutch at this time, many Englishmen continued to resent Dutch fishing off their coasts. This friction soon spread to other waters. In 1613, James granted the Muscovy Company an exclusive monopoly of the whale fishery in Spitzbergen, claiming those waters as part of the British seas. The Dutch replied in 1614 by establishing a rival Northern Company, basing their claim on the right of discovery.

INTRODUCTION

In other areas of trade, disputes arose in England over the exportation of dyed cloth to the Dutch Republic. In response, the Dutch forbade the English to export them to the Republic in 1615. At the same time, there had been disagreements over trade rights in the East Indies; there the Dutch prevented the English from sharing trade in the Banda Islands, Amboyna, and the Moluccas. In 1615, the Dutch and English began negotiations to try to arrange cooperation between the two rival East India companies.

Thus, in 1614 and 1615 as these four pamphlets appeared, there was friction, but as yet little open hostility with the Dutch. Just beginning to move outward with success in the East Indies trade and with new colonies in America, England was becoming more concerned with her policy of "sovereignty of the sea" at home. Many Englishmen were beginning to see dangers in the rivalry from the Dutch fishing fleet and quickly linked it to other issues, such as the freedom of the seas, whaling, East India trade, and even the cloth trade. The four pamphlets in this collection reflect the crosscurrents of these issues.

England's Way to Win Wealth

Tobias Gentleman wrote the first of these four pamphlets, *England's Way to Win Wealth*. The publisher, Nathaniel Butter,[3] registered it for publication at the Stationers' Office[4] on 28 January 1614, although the last page of the pamphlet bears the date 18 February.

We know little about the author, beyond what he tells us in the pamphlet. In a marginal note, we learn that his father lived in Sowld or Southwold, until he was 98 years old, where he worked for many years in the Ling fishery.

INTRODUCTION

Located near Great Yarmouth, Norfolk, the town was one of its four member ports on the North Sea coast.[5] Gentleman is not known to have written anything else, but Edward Sharpe, the reputed author of *Britaine's Busse*, gives a further hint when he notes that he had heard that Gentleman "was trained up from his youth, and is very expert, both in navigation and fishing."[6]

The English herring fishing industry expanded greatly in the late sixteenth and early seventeenth centuries. From the very beginning, there was much attention paid to the rivalry with the Dutch and it was common to find the statistics on the extent of the Dutch trade greatly exaggerated. Many historians emphasized the views found in an essay that received widespread attention through its attribution to Sir Walter Ralegh[7] or those in another essay by John Keymer.[8] In 1911, Thomas Fulton showed that these, in fact, were two versions of the same work by Keymer, originally written in 1605 or 1606, revised and resubmitted in 1620 to the King.[9] In contrast to Keymer, Gentleman's statistics are moderate and Fulton concluded that Gentleman's pamphlet was a more honest account of the facts. Seen in the light of the discussion over the dating and authorship of Keymer's work, it is interesting that Gentlemen mentions that he had reviewed some of Keymer's work:

> It was my fortune, some two years past, to be sent for into the company of one master John Keymar . . . and showed unto me some few notes that he had gathered and gotten from other men of my trade.[10]

The general argument that Gentlemen makes is typical of those who believed that the first step for England to take in becoming a wealthy nation was to secure the fisheries.

INTRODUCTION

After that she could securely move out into wider areas of shipping and maritime commerce. Like others trying to encourage the herring fishery, Gentleman believed that Englishmen should follow the pattern of the Dutch. For this reason, he added as an appendix a translation of one of the Dutch proclamations from the 1580s on herring fishing. In publishing it, he wanted to stir resentment about Dutch policy and suggest that England adopt similar measures to protect its own fishing industry. Like many others, he thought that the king should put his proclamation into effect. At the same time, he wanted to encourage English-built fishing ships, and even offered to supply the appropriate dimensions for such vessels to anyone who applied to him, "because I know that the ship carpenters of England, be not yet skilful in this matter."[11]

In trying to promote the English herring industry, private individuals were seeking special privileges and immunities. In December 1611, one group of individuals formed a corporation that imitated the Dutch approach. Among other things, they asked that they be allowed to carry their fish to foreign ports and to bring back foreign commodities in exchange. This automatically put the fishermen into rivalry with the major trading groups, such as the Merchant Adventurers, the Muscovy Company, the Levant Company, and The East India Company, which wanted to preserve their trading privileges.

Historians have widely used Gentleman's pamphlet. After a reprint in 1660, it appeared in the eighteenth century in the *Harleian Miscellany*[12] and, in the nineteenth century it was reprinted again by Edward Arber.[13] When it was first published in 1614, it began a public debate on some of the issues surrounding the herring fishery.

INTRODUCTION

The Trade's Increase

On 12 February 1615, Walter Burre and Nicholas Okes[14] registered a pamphlet with the Company of Stationers in London, *The Trade's Increase*.[15] This was the first pamphlet to pick up and expand on the argument in *England's Way to Win Wealth*.

Published anonymously, the note "To the reader" ends with the initials "I. R." or "J. R." There has been a long controversy over the identity of the author. Some scholars interpreted these as the initials of one John Roberts, who some then listed as the author of the pamphlet, while others continued to used the initials alone. The introductory note, however, is worded in a manner suggesting that its author was not the author of the pamphlet. In addition, it is possible that the initials are not even those of the preface writer, but merely a reference to the king, Jacobus Rex. The only direct clue in the pamphlet is the author's passing comment on the last page of the pamphlet: "I was born in the City, and live amongst seamen."[16] Nevertheless, the arguments in the pamphlet led the government to the author.

The author surveyed the range of English maritime trade and argued that the fisheries based in England should be increased. He saw little value in the future of American trade, and argued that England merchants should develop further a free trade on the pattern already well established with Germany, the Baltic, the Low Countries, Spain, Portugal, and the Mediterranean.

In light of these issues, the very title of the pamphlet drew public attention to a recent disaster for the East India Company. In 1611, the East India Company's sixth voyage had sailed. There were only three ships, but the largest of

INTRODUCTION

them was the 1,100-ton Company-built ship named *Trade's Increase*. The voyage proved to be a hazardous and unprofitable one. Failing to establish a factory at Surat, the commander, Sir Henry Middleton, moved on to the Red Sea and Aden, where he became a prisoner for a time. Later, while under repair near Bantam, *Trade's Increase* burned, a total loss.[17] Thus, the pamphlet's title clearly suggested an attack on the East India Company, charging that the East India Company had lost too many valuable ships and cargoes. In addition, the author complained that the Company's emphasis on the construction of such large ships damaged the medium size ship-building industry in England. Besides, the East India Company's spice trade forced the cost of spices up for other traders, particularly for the Levant Company that purchased its spices from Arab sources. Most importantly, the East India Company was responsible for exporting bullion and thereby depleting the nation's supply of a vital element in the balance of free trade.

This attack on the East India Company was enough to have its author temporarily sent to the Fleet Prison, but it was not until 1934 that the well-known historian of the East India Company, William Foster, brought attention to the published documents that told the story and proved that the author was Robert Kayll.[18]

On 16 February 1615, just four days after the publisher registered the pamphlet, the Court minutes of the East India Company record that the Directors consulted the Archbishop of Canterbury about the offensive pamphlet. The Archbishop promised that the pamphlet would be suppressed, but advised the Company not to take any direct notice of the pamphlet's criticism. The Court appointed two of its members to study the pamphlet further and to report

INTRODUCTION

whether they thought Star Chamber proceedings would be in order. Six days later, they reported that lawyers had found several points close to treason and that all the rest was very dangerous. In the light of this, the Court decided to ask for further advice from the Solicitor-General. On 29 March, the Minutes allude to the disgrace brought upon the Company by "the unjust writings of Keale."[19]

On 4 April 1615, the Privy Council, which included the Archbishop of Canterbury among its members, met and examined Kayll on charges connected with the pamphlet. Failing to receive any satisfaction, the Privy Council issued

> A warrant to the Warden of the Fleet to receave into his charge and custodye the person of Robert Keale, and him there to deteyne until he receave further order concernying him.[20]

Nearly two weeks later, on 17 April, Kayll wrote the following petition, acknowledging his offence:

> To the Right Honorable the Lords of his Majesties most honorable Privy Council
>
> The humble petition of Robert Kaylle
>
> Sheweth that whereas it pleased your Lordships to command the said petitioner before you, concerning a late treatise written by him, in answering whereof, for that he neither gave satisfaction to your Lordships by this correccion upon him.
>
> Now may it please your Lordships, upon this humble suite and submission, wherein he very justly condemneth himself, to pardon there his transgressions and to release him of

INTRODUCTION

this his deserved punishment and imprisonment, whereby (but chiefly by your Lordship's most wise and just reprehensions) he is truely and, as he hopeth, sufficiently admonished both of his duty to the commonwealth and your lordships, to whose mercy he most humblie submits himselfe.

Subscribed as by the submission it selfe appeareth, the 17 April 1615.

The treatise before mentioned is called *The Trades Increase*.

Robert Kayll[21]

Upon receipt of this petition, the Privy Council was satisfied and issued another warrant, setting Kayll free:

A Warrant to the Warden of the Fleete

Whereas Robert Kayll was heretofore committed unto that prison of the Fleete there to remayne until you should receave further order concernying him and for as much as we have now thought fitting of his humble submission and acknowledgement of his offence, he be released of his imprisonment; These are therefore to will and command you forthwith to sett at liberty the said Robert Kayll, paying his fees, for which this shall be your sufficient warrant.[22]

The official records remain silent about the pamphlet for two years, until 1617 when the Court of the East India Company considered the appointment of a chief commander at Bantam. While criticizing much of the East India Company's work, *The Trade's Increase* had heaped praise on the

INTRODUCTION

success of Thomas Best and the 1612 voyage under his command. This passage seems to have been what lay in the minds of the members of the East India Court, when Best appeared as the most qualified man for the post at Bantam. During the debate in the Court over his appointment,

> others advised to consider how safelye they may employe him, who regards not his bond nor promise, having been ungrateful and opposite against the Company since his retourne, prowde, and suspected to have had a hand in Keales booke. But as all men have their imperfections so he hath his.[24]

Meanwhile *The Trade's Increase* received a wide circulation. The surviving copies appear in three different states, suggesting that it went through at least three different printings. Additionally, it appeared again in the eighteenth century in the *Harleian Miscellany*.[25]

The Defence of Trade

While the Archbishop of Canterbury had advised the directors of the East India Company to bide their time and make no initial public response to the *Trade's Increase,* the Company's patience was strained to the limit. Even before Kayll's appearance at the Privy Council, John Barnes had registered *The Defence of Trade* for the printer William Stansby[26] at the Company of Stationers on 21 March 1615.[27] Written as a letter to the Governor of the East India Company, Sir Thomas Smith, the author, Sir Dudley Digges, notes that he had first thought the pamphlet worthy only of the Company's contempt, but upon reading it over found that gilded over with that commendable proposition of the herring fishing, a sort of pills are put to swallowing that perhaps may worke weak stomacks to distaste our Course of Traffick by societies in London.[28]

Sir Dudley Digges was a powerful and informed defender of the East India Company. He came from a well-known family with a long association in maritime affairs. He was the grandson of Leonard Digges who had studied at University College, Oxford, and been a close friend of John Dee's. Leonard had made refracting telescopes as early as the 1550s, written a popular calendar with tide and altitude tables entitled *Prognostication*, and also adapted the geometrical square for seamen's use. Leonard's son and Dudley's father, Thomas Digges, had studied at Queen's College, Cambridge, and had been a pupil of Dee's. Thomas Digges had been a member of parliament for Wallingford in 1572 and for Southampton in 1585. He served as muster-master-general of English forces in the Netherlands in 1586. With others, he had been commissioned in 1590 to equip an expedition for exploration of the Arctic and Cathay, and he was one of the first English mathematicians to go to sea and to write several books on navigation.[29]

Dudley Digges was born at the family seat, Digges Court at Barham, Kent, in 1583 and matriculated at University College, Oxford, at the age of 17 in July 1600. He graduated as a bachelor of arts in 1601. In 1604, he was joint author with his father of *Foure Paradoxes or Politique Discourses*. A courtier, Dudley Digges was knighted by James I at Whitehall in 1607, and he became a member of parliament for Tewkesbury in 1610, a seat to which he was re-elected in 1614, 1621, 1624, 1625, and 1626. He was an early shareholder of the East India Company. At the age of 27, he be-

INTRODUCTION

came one of the principal English promoters of Henry Hudson's fourth voyage. Passionately interested in this project, John Chamberlain wrote in 1611 to Sir Dudley Carleton, that the plans did not "give him leave to thincke of anything els, for yt possesseth him wholy."[31] It was on this voyage in search of the Northwest passage that Hudson entered the narrow passage that led to the great bay that bears his name, naming the island on the northern side of the passage, Digges Island. In 1612, Digges was a founder of "the Company of Merchants of London, Discoverers of the Northwest Passage," which later supported the northern voyages of Luke Foxe, Thomas James, Robert Bylot, and William Baffin. In 1612, Digges was a possible candidate for secretary of state, and in 1614, he had been a candidate for Governor of the East India Company.

Using data that he had obtained from the East India Company records, Digges defended the Company's trading practices and showed that Kayll had exaggerated the Company's losses in *The Trade's Increase*. He showed that these losses took place during the very early voyages, not the more recent ones. In rebuttal to Kayll's criticism of exporting bullion, Digges argued that the bullion he referred to was, in fact, Spanish coin bought in the Netherlands and paid for in English commodities. Thus, he argued, it created a net gain, not a loss. Recent historians have pointed out, however, that Digges exaggerated this point. It was a new idea and would take a long time to become the standard practice for the Company.[32]

Digges's pamphlet became well known. In the nineteenth century, one commentator wrote, "It contains some curious particulars, but wants the ingenuity and originality of [Thomas] Mun's tract."[33]

INTRODUCTION

In 1616, Digges became involved in a dispute with his publisher and printer about *The Defence of Trade*. The records of the Court of the Stationer's Company provide no hints about the issues, but merely state for 21 June 1616:

> Where there are certain differences between Mr Wm Stansby and Jo Barnes about printing Sir Dudley Digges his book, nowe all matters in question are referred by order of a Court and Consent of both partyes to Mr [William] Jaggarde and Mr [Anthony] Gijlmyn [Gilman], and in the meane time are suite to stay.[34]

Interestingly, Jaggard published the final pamphlet in this series.

Britaine's Busse

William Jaggard and Nicholas Bourne registered *Britaine's Busse* at the Stationer's Office on 10 May 1615,[35] some six weeks after *The Defence of Trade* appeared.

The only hint in the pamphlet to the author are the initials E. S., which scholars attribute to one Edward Sharpe. Referring to both Tobias Gentleman's *England's Way to Win Wealth* and to Kayll's *The Trade's Increase,* as well as to much earlier works from the 1570s and '80s, he returns the argument to the original theme, the development of the English herring fishery. In doing so, he notes,

> I think the East India company will liberally further this work: for that thereby some of their greatest wants are like to be supplied.
> I speake as I think without insinuation, which I hate as much as rayling.[36]

INTRODUCTION

Fifteen years later, the pamphlet reappeared under the title *England's Royall Fishing Ruined,* but with the identical sub-title.[37]

Britaine's Busse adds much interesting detail, complementing the material on the herring fishery found in *The Trade's Increase* and *England's Way to Win Wealth,* even repeating from Gentleman's pamphlet, the Dutch proclamation "as a thing to be often seene and considered of us".

Taken together as a sustained debate, these four pamphlets show the range of political considerations involved in developing the English herring fishery and show how these fisheries came into opposition with the great trading companies. Simultaneously, one can find in them the cross-currents involved in Anglo-Dutch rivalry, the development of the East India Company, and gain a general impression of English trade patterns at this time along with detailed information on the herring fishery.

John B. Hattendorf
Naval War College

NOTES

1. Ralph Davis, *The Rise of the English Shipping Industry* (Newton Abbott, 1972), p. 9.

2. Printed in full in Thomas Wemyss Fulton, *The Sovereignty of the Sea: An Historical Account of the Claims of England to the Dominion of the British Seas, and of the Evolution of the Territorial Waters; with Special Reference to the Rights of Fishing and the Naval Salute* (Edinburgh and London, 1911; Rpt. Milwood, N.Y., 1976), Appendix F, pp. 755-756.

3. A bookseller as well as a printer, he was active from 1604 to 1640.

4. Edward Arber, *A Transcript of the Registers of the Company of Stationers of London* (London, 1876), volume 3, p. 540. STC 11745. The register uses Old Style dates, thus the entry is dated January 1613.

5. T. S. Willan, *The English Coasting Trade 1600-1750*. (Manchester, 1938), pp. 129-132.

6. *Britaine's Busse*, p. 1.

7. "*Observations Touching Trade and Commerce with the Hollander, and with other Nations, presented to King James, wherein is proved that our Sea and Land Commodities serve to enrich and strengthen other countries against our own,*" in Sir Walter Raleigh, *Collected Works*, (Oxford, 1829), vol. viii, pp. 351 ff.

8. *Observations made upon the Dutch Fishing about the year 1601. Demonstrating that there is more Wealth raised out of Herrings and other Fish in his Majesty's Seas, by the neighboring Nations in One Year, then the King of Spain hath from the Indies in Four*. London, Printed from the Original Manuscript for Sir Edward Ford, in the year 1664.

9. Thomas Wemyss Fulton, *The Sovereignty of the Sea*, pp. 126-129. See also, "Introduction" to M. F. Lloyd Prichard, ed., *Original papers Regarding Trade in England and Abroad Drawn up by John Keymer* (New York, 1967) and

Pierre Le Franc, *Sir Walter Ralegh, Ecrivain, l'oeuvre et les idées* (Paris, 1968).

10. *England's Way to Win Wealth*, pp. 3-4.
11. *England's Way to Win Wealth*, p. 46.
12. *The Harleian Miscellany* (London, 1744-1746), volume 4, p. 403 ff.
13. Edward Arber, ed. *An English Garner: Ingatherings from our history and literature* (Birmingham, 1882), volume 4, pp. 323-352. Also published on microfilm in Goldsmiths'-Kress Library of Economic Literature (1974), no. 429.
14. Walter Burre was a bookseller; Nicholas Okes was a printer active from 1606 to 1645. In other publications, Okes sometimes used a Latin form of his name, Derwent de Quercubus.
15. Arber, ed. *Registers*, volume 3, p. 563. Formerly STC 20579, renumbered in second edition of STC 14894.7.
16. *The Trades Increase*, p. 56.
17. A. D. Innes, *The Maritime and Colonial Expansion of England under the Stuarts (1603-1714)* (London, 1932), pp. 64, 67; Kenneth R. Andrews, *Trade, Plunder and Settlement* (Cambridge, 1984), pp. 24, 271.
18. William Foster, "Letter to the Editor: The Author of 'The Trade's Increase'," *The Times Literary Supplement*, 29 March 1934, p. 229. The documents spell the name alternatively as "Keale", "Kaylle", and "Kayll", but he signed his name "Kayll".
19. *Ibid.*
20. *Acts of the Privy Council of England 1615-1616* (London, 1925), p. 99.
21. *Ibid.*, p. 108.
22. *Ibid.*, p. 107.
23. *The Trade's Increase*, pp. 29-30.

INTRODUCTION

24. Court Minutes 10 October 1617 (volume iv, p. 32), excerpt printed in Sir William Foster, ed., *The Voyage of Thomas Best* (Hakluyt Society, second series, volume lxxv, 1934), pp. 295-296. For a revision to Sir John Knox Laughton's biography of Best in the *Dictionary of National Biography*, volume 4, pp. 418-20, including corrected birth and death dates (c. 1657-1639), see Foster's introduction to the above.

25. (London, 1744), volume 4, pp. 212-231. Variant copies of the original are also published on microfilm in the Goldsmiths'-Kress Library of Economic Literature (1974), nos. 438 and 439, and by University Microfilms International, in the series Early English Books, 1475-1640 (1984), from an original in the Cambridge University Library (1984), v 1797:4 and in the same series from the University of Illinois Library at Urbana-Champaign (1985), 1835:8.

26. Stansby was active as a printer between 1597 and 1639.

27. Arber, ed. *Registers*, volume 3, p. 565. STC 6845. A facsimile edition appeared in *The English Experience, its record in early printed books published in facsimile* (Amsterdam: Theatrum Orbis Terrarum; New York: Da Capo Press, c. 1968). A microfilm edition appears in the Goldsmiths'-Kress Library of Economic Literature (1974), no. 436.

28. *The Defence of Trade*, pp. 1-2.

29. On Leonard Digges, see E. G. R. Taylor, *The Haven-Finding Art* (New York, 1957), pp. 197-199, 205 and D. W. Waters, *The Art of Navigation in England in Elizabethan and Early Stuart Times* (New Haven, 1958), pp. 96-97, 127-128, 149-150, 186, 225, 245, 298, 341-343, 471, 497.

On Thomas Digges, see Taylor, pp. 205-206, 210, 215, 219 and Waters, pp. 96-98, 125, 143-144, 149-150, 225, 245, 298, 304-305, 533-534, 584.

INTRODUCTION

30. Joseph Foster, *Alumni Oxoniensis: The Members of the University of Oxford 1500-1714*, volume 1, p. 403, and the *Dictionary of National Biography*.

31. Quoted in Kenneth R. Andrews, *Trade, Plunder and Settlement* (Cambridge, 1984), p. 346.

32. Quinn and Ryan, *England's Sea Empire*, p. 160.

33. Quoted from *McCulloch's Literature of Political Economy* in S. Austin Allibone, *A Critical Dictionary of English Literature* and *British and American Authors*. . . . (London, 1877), p. 503. The reference is to Mun's pamphlet *A Discourse of Trade, from England unto the East Indies* (London, 1621).

34. W. A. Jackson, ed. *Records of the Court of the Stationer's Company: Court Book C*, p. 87.

35. STC 21486. Published on microfilm in the Goldsmiths'-Kress Library of Economic Literature (1974), no. 435.

36. *Britaine's Busse*, F2v.

37. (1630) STC 21487. Published on microfilm in Goldsmiths'-Kress Library of Economic Literature (1974), no. 605.

FURTHER READING

For general studies on the development of English maritime affairs, see:

Andrews, Kenneth R., *Trade, Plunder and Settlement: Maritime Enterprise and the Genesis of the British Empire 1480-1630* (Cambridge, 1984)

Davis, Ralph, *The Rise of the English Shipping Industry* (London, 1972).

Quinn, D. B., and A. N. Ryan, *England's Sea Empire, 1550-1642*. Early Modern Europe Today series. (London, 1983).

Willan, T. S., *English Coasting Trade 1600-1750*, Publications of the University of Manchester, cclxiv; Economic History series, xii (Manchester, 1938).

For Anglo-Dutch rivalry, see:

Edmondson, G., *Anglo-Dutch Rivalry During the First Half of the Seventeenth Century being the Ford Lectures Delivered at Oxford in 1910*. (Oxford: At the Clarendon Press, 1911.)

Fulton, Thomas Wemyss, *The Sovereignty of the Sea: An Historical Account of the Claims of England to the Dominion of the British Seas, and of the Evolution of the Territorial Waters: with Special Reference to the Rights of Fishing and the Naval Salute* (Edinburgh and London: William Blackwood and Sons, 1911; Rpt. Milwood, N.Y.: Kraus Reprint Co., 1976).

Haley, K. H. D., *The British and the Dutch: Political and Cultural Relations Through the* Ages (London, 1988).

INTRODUCTION

For further details on the herring fishery, see:

Bruce, R. Stuart, "The Haaf Fishing and Shetland Trading," *Mariner's Mirror,* volume 8 (1922), pp. 48-52.

—————, "Note: Herring Fishing on the Coast of Shetland [1718]," *Mariner's Mirror,* volume 8 (1922), pp. 26-27.

—————, "Shetland and the Dutch War 1781," *Mariner's Mirror,* volume 37 (1951), pp. 282-292.

Jenkins, James Travis, *The Herring and Herring Fisheries.* (London, P. S. King and Son, 1927.)

Mitchell, A. R., "The European Fisheries in Early Modern History," in E. E. Rich and C. H. Wilson, eds., *The Cambridge Economic History of Europe,* volume 5 (Cambridge, 1977), pp. 134-184.

Samuel, Arthur Michael, *The Herring; Its Effect on the History of Britain.* (London: John Murray, 1918.)

On the East India Company, see:

Foster, William, *England's Quest of Eastern Trade* (London, 1933).

—————, ed., *The Voyage of Thomas Best.* Hakluyt Society, 2nd series, lxxv (London, 1934).

GENTLEMAN, TOBIAS.

Englands way to win wealth, and to employ ships and marriners: or, a plaine description what great profite, it will bring vnto the common-wealth of England ... With a true relation of the inestimable wealth that is yearely taken out of His Maiesties seas, by the Hollanders ... And also a discourse of the sea-coast townes of England ... By Tobias Gentleman, fisherman and marriner.

London printed for Nathaniel Butter. 1614.

Collation: 18 cm. (4to): A^4 (-A4) B-G^4 H^2 (-H2). [6], 46, [4] p.; coat of arms.

Notes: Pages 17, 33, 36, 37, 40 misnumbered 19, 27, 26, 31, 30 respectively. "The States proclamation, translated out of the Dutch", p. [1-4] at end. Mentions "discouery of the West Indies" on p. [5], 1st count.

References: JCB Lib. cat., pre-1675, II, p. 102; JCB Lib. *Maritime history,* 457; Alden, J. E. *European Americana,* 614/40.

JCB Library copy: Acq: 07982. Acquired before 1874. This copy lacks p. 17-24 (gathering D); facsimiles from the copy in the Houghton Library at Harvard are here inserted. Bound with: Kayll, Robert. The trades increase. London, 1615, and with: Digges, Dudley, Sir. The defence of trade. London, 1615. Call number: D614 G338e.

Tracings: 1. Fisheries—Great Britain. 2. Herring fisheries—Great Britain. 3. Fishery law and legislation—Netherlands. I. Title. II. Title: A plaine description what great profite it will bring. III. United Provinces of the Netherlands. Staten Generaal.

KAYLL, ROBERT.

The trades increase.

London, printed by Nicholas Okes, and are to be sold by Walter Burre. 1615.

Collation: 18 cm. (4to): A^4 (-A4) B-H^4. [6], 56 p.

Notes: "To the reader" signed (p. 5): I. R.; ascribed incorrectly to John Roberts. Authorship based on William Foster, "The author of 'The trades increase'," *London Times Literary Supplement,* 29 March 1934, p. 229. Three states noted: in one state the catchword on the recto of leaf B3 is "this" and line 12 of leaf G1 recto contains the word "conceipt"; in a second state these words are "new" and "conceit"; in a third state the words appear as "new," (with comma) and "coceipt". Includes references to Newfoundland, Bermuda, and Virginia.

References: JCB Lib. cat., pre-1675, II, p. 109; Alden, J. E. *European Americana,* 615/74.

JCB Library copies: Copy 1 acq: 07983. Acquired before 1874. This copy has the characteristics of the second state noted above; bound with: Gentleman, Tobias. Englands way to win wealth. London, 1614, and with: Digges, Dudley, Sir. The defence of trade. London, 1615. Call number: D614 G338e. Copy 2 acq: 02622. Acquired in 1851. This copy is bound separately and has the characteristics of the third state noted above. Call number: D615 K23t.

Tracings: 1. Great Britain—Commerce. 2. East India Company. 3. Herring fisheries—Great Britain. I. Title. II. J. R. (John Roberts).

DIGGES, DUDLEY, SIR, 1583-1639.

The defence of trade. In a letter to Sir Thomas Smith Knight, gouernour of the East-India Compagnie, &c. From one of that societie.

London, printed by William Stansby for Iohn Barnes, and are to be sold at his shop ouer against Saint Sepulchres Church without Newgate. 1615.

Collation: 18 cm. (4to): [A]^2 (-[A]2) B-G^4 H^2. [2], 50, [2] p.

Notes: Letter signed (p. 50): Dudly Digges. Reply to: Kayll, Robert. The trades increase. London, 1615. Page 9 misnumbered 6. Includes references to Virginia.

References: JCB Lib. cat., pre-1675, II, p. 107; Alden, J. E. *European Americana*, 615/47.

JCB Library copy: Acq: 07984. Acquired before 1874. This copy is bound with: Gentleman, Tobias. Englands way to win wealth. London, 1614, and with: Kayll, Robert. The trades increase. London, 1615. Call number: D614 G338e.

Tracings: 1. East India Company. 2. Kayll, Robert. Trades increase. I. Title. II. Smith, Thomas, Sir, 1559?- 1625.

SHARPE, EDWARD, 17TH CENT.

Britaines busse. Or a computation aswell of the charge of a busse or herring-fishing ship. As also of the gaine and profit thereby. With the States proclamation annexed vnto the same, as concerning herring-fishing. By E. S.

London, printed by William Iaggard for Nicholas Bourne, and are to be sold at his shop at the south entry of the Royal Exchange. 1615.

Collation: 20 cm. (4to): A-F^4 (F4 verso blank). [48] p.

Notes: Two states noted: with or without errata statement after "Finis". Reference to timber from "Virginia and Sommer-Islands" on p. [38]. "The States proclamation translated out of Dutch", p. [45-47].

References: Alden, J. E. *European Americana,* 615/115; JCB Lib. *Maritime history,* 458.

JCB Library copy: Acq: 76-108. Acquired in 1976. This copy does not have the errata statement after "Finis". Call number: 76-108.

Tracings: 1. Fishing boats—Great Britain. 2. Herring fisheries—Great Britain. I. Title. II. Title: A computation as well of the charge of a busse or herring-fishing ship. III. United Provinces of the Netherlands. Staten Generaal.

Englands
VVAY TO VVIN
Wealth, and to employ Ships
and Marriners.

OR,

A plaine description what great profite, it will bring vnto the Common-wealth of *England*, by the Erecting, Building, and aduenturing of Busses, to Sea, a fishing.

With a true Relation of the inestimable wealth that is yearely taken out of his Maiesties Seas, by the Hollanders, by their great numbers of Busses, Pinkes, and Line-boates:

And Also

A discourse of the Sea-coast Townes of England, and the most fit and commodious places, and Harbours that wee haue for Busses, and of the small number of our Fishermen, and also the true valuation, and whole charge, of Building, and Furnishing, to Sea, Busses, and Pinks, after the Holland manner.

By *Tobias Gentleman*, Fisherman and Marriner.

LONDON
Printed By *Nathani-l Butter.* 1614.

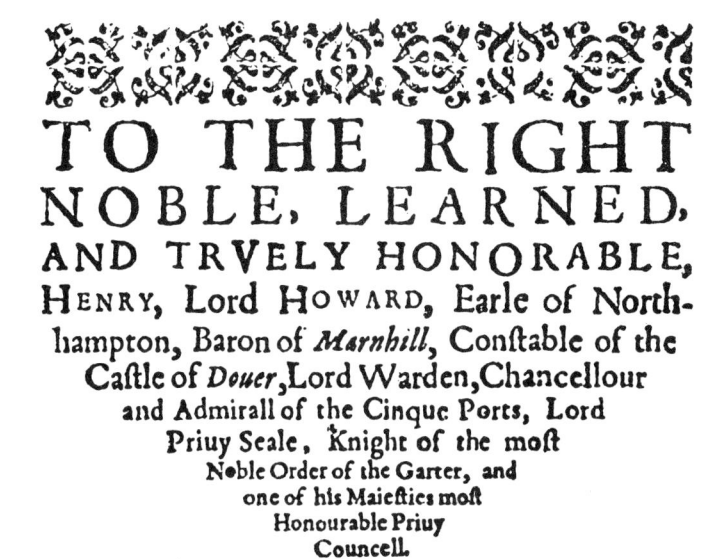

TO THE RIGHT NOBLE, LEARNED, AND TRVELY HONORABLE,

HENRY, Lord HOWARD, Earle of Northhampton, Baron of *Marnhill*, Constable of the Castle of *Douer*, Lord Warden, Chancellour and Admirall of the Cinque Ports, Lord Priuy Seale, Knight of the most Noble Order of the Garter, and one of his Maiesties most Honourable Priuy Councell.

RIGHT HONOVRABLE,

Seeing that by Nature our Country challengeth a greater interest in vs, then our Parents, Friends, or Children can, and that we ought for preseruation thereof, oppose our liues vnto the greatest dangers: It is

the

The Epistle

the part of euery Natiue to endeauor something to the aduancement and profite thereof, and not to affect it, for that wee possesse in it, but to loue it for it selfe, as being the common Mother and Nourisher of vs all. For mine owne part, albeit my short fadome can compasse no such great designe as I desire, yet from a willing minde (as hee that offerd his hands full of water to great Artaxerxes) I am bold to present this proiect of my honest and homely labours, beseeching your L. whose vertues haue truely enobled you, to take the same into your protection: And prefer it to the veiw of our most Royall Soueraigne, recommending the good effecting thereof to his gracious fauor and furtherance. Doubtlesse your actions and endeauours hauing

all

DEDICATORY.

all bene full of virtue and goodnesse, are not the least preuailing motiues whereby his Maiesty hath so endeered you vnto him. In this then you shall not thinke your selfe disparaged, the matter being both honest and commendable, and in true valew of as great substance, as the offer of Sebastian Cabota, *to King Henry the seuenth, for the discouery of the West Indies.*

Humbly at your Lordships
commandement,

Tobias Gentleman.

I R

ENGLANDS WAY TO WIN WEALTH, AND TO IMploy Ships and Marriners.

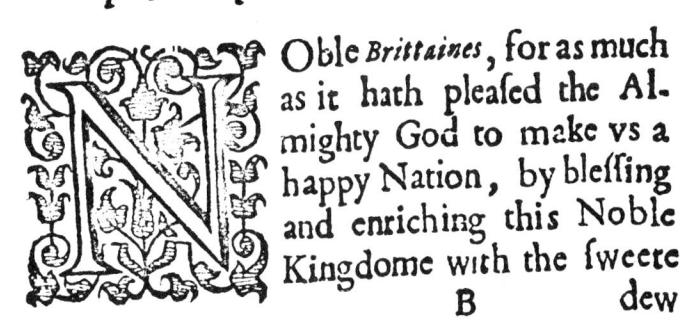

Noble *Brittaines*, for as much as it hath pleased the Almighty God to make vs a happy Nation, by blessing and enriching this Noble Kingdome with the sweete dew

dew of his heauenly word, truely and plentifully Preached amongſt vs; and alſo in cytuating our Country in a moſt wholeſom Clymate, & ſtored with many rich & pleaſant Treaſures for our benefite, which alſo yeeldeth in aboundance all things neceſſary, ſo that wee doe not onely excel other Nations in ſtrength & courage, but alſo all other Kingdomes far remote are by our Engliſh comodities releiued & cheriſhed. It ſeemeth that the wiſedome of our gracious God, hath reſerued vs as ſome pretious gemme vnto himſelfe in invironing our Country with the plenteous Ocean Sea, & diuiding of vs frō the whole Continent of the reſt of the inferiour world, by our rich and commodious Element of water, which in due ſeaſons yeeldeth to vs in aboundance. For although our Champion Soile, by the dilligence of the Husbandman, be plentifull vnto vs: yet doth theſe watry Regions and Dominions yeeld yearely, great variety of all kind of moſt wholeſome and dainty fiſhes: ſo that it may ſeeme ſtrange and diſputable, and hard to determine, which of his Maieſties Dominions of the Land or Seas, bee richeſt. My ſelfe being the moſt vnworthieſt of
all,

all, in that I am no Sholler, but borne a Fishermans sonne by the Sea-side, and spending my youthfull time at Sea about Fisher affaires, whereby now I am more skilfull in Nets, Lines, and Hookes, then in Rethoricke, Logicke, or learned bookes: yet in those fewe which I haue read, besides the instinct of nature, which maketh me to know that euery one should endeuour himselfe the best he is able to be beneficiall & profitable to the Kingdome & Common-wealth wherein hee is borne, which was a forceable motiue to incite me to thinke of this present discourse, the penning whereof was thus occasioned.

It was my fortune, some two yeares past, to bee sent for into the company of one Maister *Iohn Keymar*, who is a man very well deseruing of his Country, and hee knowing me to haue experience in Fisher affaires, demanded of me the charge both of Busses and Line-boates, after the Hollanders fashion, and shewed vnto mee some few notes that hee had gathered and gotten from other men of my trade, which hee seemed greatly to esteeme of: for that himselfe was altogether vnexperimented in such busi-nesse,

nesse, and further, I deliuered to him certaine principall notes which hee seemed greatly to esteeme; for that hee said that hee did mind to shew them vnto the right Honourable Counsell, whereupon I entred into the cogitation of writing this true relation out of my owne experience and knowledge, touching the Inestimable summes of money taken yearely for fish and herrings out of his Maiesties Seas by strangers, whereby they haue not onely maintained their warres many yeares against the Spaniard, both by Land & Sea, he being one of the great Monarkes of the world, and at length, they haue not onely wearied him in the wars, and brought him to good termes & reasonable composition; but also it is most apparant notwithstanding the huge charge of their warres so long continued, which would haue made any other Nation poore and beggarly, they to the contrary are growne exceeding rich and strong in fortified Townes and beautifull Buildings, in plenty of money and gold, in trade and trafficke with all other Nations, and haue so increased and multiplied their shipping and Marriners, that all other Nations and Countries in the world doe admire

admire them.

Moreouer, whereas one Hauen in one of their Townes did in former times containe their ſhips and ſhipping with infinite coſt, now they haue cut out two Hauens more to a Towne, and at this preſent, are all three Hauens ſcarce ſufficient with roome enough to containe their Ships and ſhipping, and by reaſon of their induſtrious Fiſher-trade, not one of their people are idle, nor none ſeene to begge amongſt them, except they bee ſome of our owne Engliſh Nation.

And what their chiefeſt trade is, or their principall gold-mine, is well knowne to all Merchants that haue vſed thoſe parts, and to my ſelfe and all Fiſhermen; namely that his Maiſties Seas is their chiefeſt, principall, and onely rich Treaſury, whereby they haue ſo long time maintained their warres, and haue ſo greatly proſpered, and enriched themſelues.

If that their little Countrey of the vnited Prouinces can doe this, as it is moſt manifeſt before our eyes they do, then what may we his Maieſties Subiects doe, if this trade of fiſhing were

were once erected among vs, wee hauing in our own Countries sufficient store of all necessaries to accomplish the like businesse. For the Hollanders haue nothing growing in their owne land for that businesse, but they are compelled to fetch all their wood, tymber, and planke, wherwith they build, & make all their Ships of, out of diuers Countries, and their iron out of other places, their Hempe & Cordige out of the Easterne Countries, their Hoopes and Barrellboords out of Norway & Sprucia, their breadcorne out of Poland, & East parts, their Mault, Barley and best double drinke from England, & also all their fish and chiefest wealth out of his Maiesties Seas.

The which they doe transport vnto the foresaid Countries, & returne for the procedue of fish and herrings, the fore-named commodities, whereby their Ships and Marriners are set on worke, and continually multiplied, and into their countries is plentifull store of money and gold daily brought, onely for the failes of fish and herrings.

And their Countrey being, as it were, a small plot of ground in comparison of great Brittaine,

Brittaine, for two of his Mareſties Counties, Suffolke and Norfolke, do equall, if not exceed, in ſpaciouſneſſe, all their Prouinces, & yet it is manifeſt, that for ſhipping and ſea faring men, all England, Scotland, France and Spaine, for quantity of ſhipping and Fiſher men cannot make ſo great a number.

Howſoeuer this may ſeeme ſtrange vnto many that doe not know it, yet doe I aſſure my ſelfe, that a great number beſides my ſelfe know I affirme nothing herein but the truth.

Wherefore ſeeing the great benefice that this buſines by the Buſſes, bonaduentures, or Fiſher-ſhips, by erecting of this profitable and new trade, which will bring plenty vnto his Maieſties kingdomes, and be for the generall good of the Common-wealth, in ſetting of many thouſands of poore people on worke, which now knowe not how to liue, and alſo for the increaſing of ſhippes and Fiſher-men, which ſhall bee imployed about the taking of fiſh & herrings out of his Maieſties own ſtreames, as alſo for the imploying of ſhips, and increaſing of Marriners, for the ſtrengthening of the Kingdome againſt all forraigne inuaſions, and

for

for the enriching of Merchants with tranſportation of Fiſh and Herrings into other Countries; and alſo for the bringing in of gold, and money, which now is growne but ſcarce, by reaſon that the Dutch and Hollanders haue ſo long time beene ſuffered to carry away our money and beſt gold for fiſh and Herrings, taken out of his Maieſties owne ſtreames, which his Maieſties owne Subiects do want (and ſtill are like to doe) if that they bee not forbidden for bringing vs of Fiſh and Herrings : And this worthy Common-wealthes buſineſſe of Buſſes foſtered and furthered by his Maieſties Honorable Councell, and the Worſhipfull and wealthy ſubiects, by putting too of their helping Aduentures now at the firſt: for that thoſe that bee now the Fiſher-men, of themſelues, be not able to beginne.

    Thoſe poore Boates and ſorry Nets that our Fiſhermen of England now haue, are all their chiefeſt wealthes, but were their ability better, they would ſoone be imploying themſelues: for that it is certaine that all the Fiſher-men of England do reioyce now at the very name and newes of building of Buſſes, with a moſt ioyfull
applaud

applaud, praying to God to further it for: what great profite and pleasure it will bring they doe well vnderstand, and I will hereafter declare.

First, I shall not neede to proue that it is lawfull for vs that bee his Maiesties owne Subiects to take with all dilligence the blessings that Almighty God doe yeerely send vnto vs at their due times and seasons, and which doe offer themselues freely and aboundantly to vs, in our owne Seas and nigh our owne shores.

Secondly, to proue that it is feacible for vs: for what can bee more plaine then that we see daily done before our eyes by the Hollanders, that haue nothing that they vse growing in their owne Land, but are constrained to fetch all out of other Countries; whereas we haue all things that shall bee vsed about that businesse growing at home in our owne Land, Pitch and Tarre onely excepted.

Thirdly, to proue it will bee profitable, no man need to doubt, for that we see the Hollanders haue long maintained their warres, and are neuerthelesse growne exceeding rich, which are
things

things to be admired, in so much that themselues do call it, their *Chiefest Trade, and principall Gold-mine, whereby many thousands of their people of Trades and Occupations, bee set on worke, well maintained, and do prosper*: These be the Hollanders owne words in a Dutch Proclamation, and translated into English, and the coppy of that Proclamation is here annexed vnto the end of my booke.

And shall wee neglect so great blessings: O slothfull England and carelesse Countrimen, Looke but on these fellowes that wee call the plumpe Hollanders, behold their dilligence in fishing, and our owne carelesse negligence.

In the midst of the month of May doth the Industrious Hollanders beginne to make ready their Busses and Fisher-fleetes, and by the first of their Iune, are they yeerly ready, and seene to saile out of the *Mase*, the *Tessell*, and the *Vly*, a thousand Saile together for to catch Herrings in the North-seas.

Sixe hundred of these Fisher-ships, and more, bee great Busses some sixe score Tunnes, most of them bee a hundreth Tunnes and the rest three score and fifty Tunnes, the biggest of them

And to imploy Ships and Marriners.

them hauing foure and twenty men, some twenty men, and some eighteene and sixteene men a peece, so that their cannot bee in this Fleete of people no lesse then twenty thousand Sailors.

These hauing with them bread, butter, and Holland-cheese, for their prouision, do daily ly get their other diet out of his Maiesties Seas, besides the lading of this Fleete three times a peece, commonly before S. *Andrew* with Herrings, which being sold by them, but at the rate of ten pound the Last, amounteth vnto much more then the summe of one million of pounds Sterling onely by this Fleete of Busses yearely: no King vpon the earth did yet euer see such a Fleete of his owne Subiects at any time, and yet this Fleete is there, and then, yearely to bee seene: A most worthy sight it were, if they were my owne Country-men, yet haue I taken pleasure in being amongst them, to behold the neatnesse of their ships and Fisher-men, how euery man knoweth his owne place, and all labouring merily together, whereby the poorest sort of themselues, their wiues, and children be well maintained, & no want seene amongst the.

And

And thus North-west and by North hence along they steere, then being the very heart of Summer, and the very yoalke of all the yeare, sayling vntill they do come vnto the Ile of Shotland, which is his Maiesties Dominions, and with these gallant Fleete of Busses, there haue bene seene twenty, thirty, and forty ships of warre to waft and gaurd them from being pillaged and taken by their enemies, and Dunkirkars: but now the warres be ended, they do saue that great charge, for they haue not now aboue foure or sixe to looke vnto them for being spoyled by Rouers and Pirates.

Shotland is the greatest Ile of all the Orcades, & lyeth in the heighth of 60. degrees of Northerly latitude.

Now if that it happen that they haue so good a winde to be at Shotland before the 14. day of their Iune, as most commonly they haue, then do they put all into Shotland, nigh Swinbornehead, into a Sownd called Braceies Sownd, and there they frolicke it on Land, vntill that they haue sucked out all the marrow of the Mault, and good Scotsh-ale, which is the best liquor that the Iland doth affoord: but the 14. day of Iune being once come, then away all of them go, for that is the first day, by their owne Law, before which time they must not lay a Net, for vntill

And to imploy Ships and Marriners.

vntill then the Herrings be not in season, nor fit to be taken to be salted.

From this place, being nigh two hundred leagues from Yermouth, do they now first begin to fish, & they do neuer leaue the Skoales of Herrings, but come along amongst them, following the Herrings as they do come, fiue hundred miles in length, and lading their ships twice or thrice, before they come to Yermouth, with the principall and best Herrings, and sending them away by the Marchant ships that cōmeth vnto them, that bringeth them victuals, barrels, and more salt, and Nets if that they do need any, the which Ships that buyeth their herrings, they do call Herring-yagers, and these Yagers carry them & sell them in the East Countries, some to *Reuell*, and to *Rie*, and some so far as the *Narue*, and *Ruffey*, *Stockhollume* in *Sweathen*, *Quinsbrough*, *Danske* and *Eluinge*, and all *Poland*, *Sprucia*, and *Pomerland*, *Letto*, *Burnt-hollume*, *Stateen*, *Lubicke* and *Youtland*, and *Denmarke*.

Returning Hemp, Flax, Cordige, Cables, and Iron, Corne, Sope-ashes, Wax, Weinskot, Clapholt, Pitch, Tarre, Mastes, and Spruce-deales, & Hoopes, and Barrel-boords, & plenty of siluer and gold onely for their procedue of Herrings.

Now besides this great Fleete of the Busses the Hollanders haue a huge number more of smaller Burthen onely for to take Herrings also, and these be of the Burthen, from fifty Tunnes vnto thirty Tunnes, and twenty tunnes; the greatest of them hauing twelue men a peece, and the smallest eight and nine men a peece, and these are Vessels of diuers fashions, and not like vnto the Busses, yet go they onely for Herrings in the season, and they bee called some of them, Sword-pinks, Flat-bottomes, Holland-toads, Crabskuits, and Yeuers, and all these, or the most part doe goe to Shot-land, but these haue no Yagers come vnto them but they go themselues home when they be laden, or else vnto the best Market: There haue bene seene and numbred of Busses, and these, in braces found, and going out to Sea, and at Sea in sight, at one time, two thousand Sailes besides them that were at Sea without sight, which could not be numbred.

It is *Bartholmew-tide* yearely before that they be come from Shotland, with the Herrings so high

And to imploy Ships and Marriners.

high as Yermouth, and all those Herrings that they doe catch in Yermouth Seas from *Bartholmew-tide* vntill *S. Andrew* the worst that be the roope-sicke Herrings that will not serue to make barreld Herrings by their owne Law, they must not bring home into Holland, wherefore they doe sell them for ready money, or gold, vnto the Yermouth-men, that be no Fisher-men, but Merchants and Ingrosers of great quantities of Herrings, if that by any meanes they can get them, so that the Hollanders be very welcome guests vnto the Yermothian Herring-buyers, and the Hollanders doe call them their Hostes, and they doe yearely carry away from Yermouth many a thousand pound, as it is wel known but, these Hollanders with their ladings of the best, which they make their best brand herrings to serue for Lenton store, they send some for *Burdeaux*, some for *Rochell*, *Nantes*, *Morliax*, and *S. Mallaus*, *Cane* in *Normandy*, *Roan*, *Paris*, *Ameancè*, and all *Pickardy*, and *Callice*, and they doe returne from these places, Wines, Salt, Fethers, Rossin, Woad, Normandy Canuise, and Dowlas cloth, and money, and French Crownes, but out of all the Arch-dukes

Countries

Countries they returne nothing from thence but ready mony, in my owne knowledge, and their ready payment was all double Iacobuses, English twenty shilling peeces. I haue seene more there in one day: then euer I did in London at any time, for at Ostend, Newport, and Dunkirke, where and when the Holland pinks commeth in, there daily the Merchants, that be but women, but not such women as the fish-wiues of Billinsgate, for these Netherland women do lade away many waggons with fresh fish daily, some for *Bridges*, and some for *Brussels*, *Iper*, *Dixmew*, and *Rissels*, and at *Sasse*, by *Gant*. I haue seene these women Merchants haue had their Apornes full of nothing but English Iacobuses, to make all their payment of, and such heapes and budget-fuls in the counting-houses of the fish-brokers, which made me much to wonder how they should come by them; and also I know that Capons are not so deerely sold by the Poulters in Gratious Streete in London, as fresh fish is sold by the Hollanders, in all those Romaine Catholicke, and Papisticall Countries.

I haue seene a small Haddocke sold there for two shillings sixe pence: and a Turbut for a Iacobus.

And whereas I haue made but a true relation

tion of their Fleetes of Busses, and onely the Herring-fishermen that be on his Maiesties Seas from Iune vntill Nouember, I will here also set downe the fishermen that all the yeare long, in the seasons, do fish for Cod and Linges continually, going and returning laden with barreld fish.

And these be Pinks and Wel-boats of the burthen of fourty Tunnes, and the smallest thirty Tunnes, and these haue some twelue men a peece, one with another, and their is of this sort of fisher-boates, beginning at *Vlushing*, *Camefere*, *Surwick-sea*, the *Mase*, the *Teffell*, & the *Fly*, and the other sandy Ilands, about fiue hundred or sixe hundred Saile, which all the yeare long are fishing for Cod, whereof they do make their barreld fish, which they do transport in Summer into the East parts, but in Winter all France is serued by them, and all the Arch-dukes Countries before spoken of, both of barreld fish, and fresh fish, which they of purpose do keepe aliue in their boates in Wells; and to vs heere in England for loue of our strong Beare, they bring vs barreld fish in Winter, and carry away our money and gold euery day

D in

in great quantities.

Besides all these Pinks and Wel boats, the Hollanders haue continually in the season, an other Fleete of Fisher-man, at the North-east head of Shotland which be of an other quality, and there is more then two hundred of these, and these be called Fly-boats, and these do ride at ankor all the season at Shotland, in the fishing grounds, and they haue small boats within them which be like vnto Cobles, the which they do put out to lay & hale their lines & hookes, whereby they do take great store of Lings, the which they do not barrell, but splet them and salt them in the Ships Bulke, and these they sell commonly for foure and fiue pounds the hundreth, and these go by the name of Holland-lings, but they are taken out of his Maiesties Seas, and were Shotland lings before they tooke them there, and for these Lings they do carry away aboundance of Englands best money daily.

Now hauing declared according vnto truth, the numbers of their Fishermen of Holland, for herrings vpon his Maiesties Seas, and also of their Pinks, and Wel-boates, and their

courses

courses for taking, and venting and selling of their barreld fish, and fresh-fish and also of their Flie-boates at the North-east head of Shotland, for Shotland-lings: I thinke it now best, truely to shew the true number of our English Fishermen, and how they do imploy themselues all the yeare long, first beginning at Colchester nigh the mouth of the Theames and so proceed Northward.

I can scarce affoord these men of that water the name of Fishermen, for that their chiefest trade is dreggin of Oisters; yet haue they in the Summer some eight or ten boates in the North-seas for Cods, which if that they happen to spend all their salt, and to speed well, they may get some twenty pound in a Summer cleere: but heere by the way, I will make knowne a great abuse that is offered to the Common-wealth, and especially to all the herring fishermen of England, onely by those men of Colchester water.

For these men from S. *Andrew* vntill *Candlemas*, & some times longer, do set forth stale-boates, amongst the sands, in the Theames mouth, for to take sprats, with great stale-nets, with a

great

great poake, and they ftanding in the Swinn: or the Kings channell on the backe of the Gunfleate, they do there take in fteed of fprats, infinite thoufands of yong Herrings, fmaller then Sprats, and not good to be eaten, for one Sprat is better worth then twenty of thofe Bleakes, or yong Herrings, but becaufe they do fill the Bufhell at Billingfgate where they do fell them for Sprats, the which, if that they were let liue, would all be at Midfummer a Fat Summer full Herring, and a pecke is fometime there fold for 2. pence which number of herrings at Midfummer, would make a barrell of Summerherrings, worth 20. or 30. fhillings.

If that they could take the Sprats it were good, for they be good victuals for the Citty, but for euery Cart-load or Bufhell of Sprats, they take a hundred Cart-loads, or Bufhels of thefe yong herrings, which be the very fpawnes of the Skoales of the herrings that commeth from Shotland euery Summer, and when as they come into Yermouth Seas yearely about S. *Luke*, and fometimes before, if that it do blow a hard Eafterly wind, do alwaies at that feafon become Roope-ficke and do

fpawne

And to imploy Ships and Marriners.

spawne and become Shotren betwixt *Winterton-nesse*, and *Orfordnesse*, and those frey of that spawne, those yong little creatures, by the wisedome of the great Creator, seeketh into the shoare, and shallow places, there to be nourished, and also into the Theames mouth into the sweetest waters; for that the water nigh the shoare, and in the Theames mouth is not so brine salt, as it is farther of into the deepe water, where these Bleakes yearely seeking to be nourished, they be alway at that season taken and destroyed: but if that these men will needs vse their stale-boates and nets, let them go where the good Sprats be, they must then stand at *Orfordnesse*, and in *Denwich-bay*, where there be cellent sprats, and for the good of all the Herring-fishermen of England, I wish that they might be prohibited to sell that which is not wholesome to be eaten, which is as much as to sell hemlocks for perseneps.

The next to Colchester, is Harwich water, a royall harbour, and a propper Towne, fit for the vse of Busses, no place in all Holland comparable, for their is both land and strand and dry beach enough for foure hundreth

Saile, but the chiefest Trade of the Inhabitants of this place, is with Caruiles for New-castle coales, but they haue three or foure Ships yearely that they do send to Isle-land for Cod and Lings, from March vntill September, and some yeares they get, and some times loose, but if that they had but once the trade of Busses, this would soone be a fine place but those Caruiles and Ships which they now haue be all their chiefest wealth.

Sixe miles vp Harwich water stands Ipswich, which is a gallant Towne, and rich: this Towne is such a place for the Busses, as in all England and Holland I know no place so conuenient: first it is the best place in all England for the building of Busses, both for the plenty of Timber and Planke, and excellent workemen for making of Ships, there is more there, then there is in sixe of the best Townes in all England: Secondly, it is a principall place for good Huswiues, for spinning of yarne, for the making of pouldauice, for there is the best that is made: which Towne with the vse of making of Twine, will soone be the best place of all England for to prouide Nets for the Busses.

It

And to imploy Ships and Marriners.

It is also a most conuenient place for the wintering of the Busses, for that all the shoares of that Riuer is altgether oose and soft ground, fit for them to lye on in winter.

Also the Ipswich men be the chiefest Marchant Aduenturers of all England for all the East-lands, for the Suffolke cloathes: and they haue their Factors lying all the yeare long in all those places where the Hollanders do vent their Herrings, and where the best price and saile is continually. And although that yet there bee no fisher-men, yet haue they store of Sea-faring men, and for Maisters for the Busses they may haue enow from *Yermouth* and *Sowld* and the Sea coast Townes downe their Riuer, from *Nacton*, and *Chimton*, *Holbroke*, *Shotly*, and *Cowines*, they may get men that will soone be good fishermen with but a little vse, for vnderstand thus much, that there is a kind of emulation in Holland betweene the Fishermen that goeth to Sea in Pinks and Line-boats, Winter and Summer, and those Fishermen that goeth in the Busses, for they in the Pinkes make a skorne of them in the Busses, & do call them *Koe-milkens*, or Cow-milkers, for in deed the most part of them

[marginal note: This Towne is a most fit and conuenient place to make a staple towne for corne, for all England, for the returne and saile of the Busses herring from Danske, and Poland]

them be men of occupations in winter, or elſe Country-men, and do milke the Cowes themſelues, and make all the Holland Cheeſe, when they be at home.

 This place is alſo moſt conuenient for the erecting of Salt-pans, for the making of Salt vpon ſalt, for that the Harbour is ſo good that at all times Ships may come vnto them with Salt from *Mayo*, or Spaniſh ſalt to make the brine or pickell, and alſo the Caruiles from New-caſtle with coales, for the boyling of it at the cheapeſt rates at any time, may come thither. To the North-eaſt of this place, three or foure leagues is *Orford-hauen*, and the Townes of *Orford* and *Alborough* eſpecially, be many good Fiſhermen, and there is belonging to thoſe Townes ſome forty or fifty North ſea boates, that yeerely goeth to Sea, hauing ſeuen men a peece, and ten or twelue Iſland Barkes, which ſometimes get ſomething, and ſometime little or nothing; if that theſe mens wealth were in Buſſes and Nets, and had but once the trade, they would put downe the Hollander, for they be great plyers of any voiage that they do vndertake.

And to imploy Ships and Marriners. 25

About three leagues to the Northward is Sowld-hauen, and in the Townes of *Sowld, don-* *wich,* and *Walderſwicke* be a very good breed of Fiſhermen, and there is belonging vnto thoſe three Townes, of North-ſea Boates ſome 20. Saile, and of Iſland Barkes ſome fifty Saile, which yearely they ſend for Cod and Lings to Iſland: This Towne of Sowld, of a Sea-coaſt Towne, is the moſt beneficiall vnto his Maieſty of all the Townes in England, by reaſon all their trade is vnto Iſland for Lings, and his Maieſties Seriant Cater hath yearely gratis, out of euery Ship and Barke, one hundreth of the choyſeſt and faireſt Lings, which be worth more then ten pound the hundred, and they call them Compoſition fiſh: But theſe men of this place, are greatly hindred, and in a manner vndone, by reaſon of their Hauen is ſo bad, and in a manner often ſtopped vp with Beach and Chingle ſtone, that the winde and the tide and the Sea do beate thether, ſo that many time, in the ſeaſon, when they be ready to go to Sea, they can not get out when time is to go to Sea, neither can they get in when they returne from Sea, but oftentimes do caſt away

Donwich in ancient times hath bene the ſeate of the Kings of the Eaſt Angles, but now all ruined.

My father liued in this Towne, vntill hee was 98. yeares of age, and gaue theſe Compoſition Lings ſeuenty yeeres, vnto foure Princes, viz. *K. Edward, Q. Mary, Q. Elizabeth,* and vntill the ſixt yeare of the raigne of our moſt gratious Soueraigne, which cometh to much more then one thouſand pound; for one man of that Towne

E their

their goods and themselues: This Hauen if that it had but a South peire built of Timber, would be a far better Hauen then Yermouth Hauen, with one quarter of the cost that hath bene bestowed on Yermouth Hauen, they be now suiters vnto his Maiestie, God grant they may speed, for it is pittifull the trouble and damage, that all the men of these three Townes do daily sustaine by their naughty Harbour.

To the North-ward of Sowld-hauen, three leagues is *Kirkley* and *Layestof* decayed Townes, they haue sixe or seuen North-sea Boates, but them of *Layestof* make benefite yearely of buying of Herrings of the Hollanders, for likewise these Hollanders be Hosted with the Layestof men, as they be with the Yermothians.

In all his Maiesties Kingdomes not any Towne comparable vnto it for braue buildings.

To the North-ward 2. leagues is the Towne of great Yermouth, very beautifully builded, vpon a very pleasant and sandy plaine of three mile in length, this Towne is a place of great resort of all the Herring fishermen of England, for thether do resort all the Fishermen of the Cinque Ports, and all the rest of the West Countrimen of England, as far as Burport and Lime

And to imploy Ships and Marriners.

Lime in Dorcetshire, and those Herrings that they do take they do not barrell, because their Boates be but small things, but they sell all vnto the Yermouth herring-buyers for ready mony, and also the Fishermen of the North-countries beyond Scarborough and Robin-hoods bay and some as far as the Bishopricke of Durham do thether resort yearely, in poore little Boates called fiue men Cobbles, & all the Herrings that they do take they do sell fresh vnto the Yermouth-men to make red Herrings. Also to Yermouth doth daily come in to the Hauen, vp to the Key, all or the most part of the great Fleet of Hollanders, which before I made relation of, that go in the *Swoard-pinks, Holland-toads, Crab-skuits, walnut shels*, and great and small *Tewers*, 100. and 200. Saile at one time together, and all their Herings that they do bring in, they do sell them all for readdy mony to the Yermouth men: And also the French men of *Pickardy* * some hundred Saile of them at a time do come thither, and all the herrings they catch they sell fresh vnto these herring mongers of Yermouth for ready gold; so that it amounteth vnto a great sum of mony, that the Hollanders & Frenchmē do cary away,

* And Normandy.

from

from Yermouth, yearely, into Holland and France, which mony doth neuer come againe into England: This Towne is very well gouerned by wife and ciuell Magiftrates, and good orders carefully obferued for the mainetenance of their Hauen and Corporation, and this Towne, by reafon of the cituation, and the frech Riuers that belongeth to it: one vp to the Citty of Norwich, and another that runneth far vp into Suffolke, a butter and cheefe country, about *Bunga* and *Betkels*; and a third that runneth far vp into Flegg, a Corne Country, by reafon whereof this Towne of Yermouth is alwaies well ferued with all kind of prouifion at all times plentifully, at good and cheape rates, whereby they of the Towne do relieue the ftrangers, and alfo do benefite themfelues: To this Towne belongeth fome twenty Ifland Barkes, which yearely they do fend for Cods and Lings, and fome hundreth and fifty Saile of North-fea boates, they make a fhift to liue, but if that they had the vfe of Buffes, and alfo barreld fifh, they would excell all England and Holland, for they be the onely fifhermen for North-feas, and alfo the beft for the handling

And to imploy Ships and Marriners.

ling of their fish that be in all this land.

The Herring buyer of Yermouth doth profite more then doth the Fishermen of Yermouth, by reason of the resort of the Hollanders, for that they are suffered to sell all their roope-sicke Herrings at Yermouth, to the Merchants there, and also the barreld fish that the Flemmings do bring in Winter to London, *Ipswich, Linne, and Hull.* do also gale them, but for that our Fishermen may, if they please, make barreld fish themselues, and therefore I will not moue them.

The Merchant herring buyer of Yermouth that hath a stocke of his owne, so long as hee can make his gaines so certaine with buying of Roope sicke herrings of the Hollanders, will neuer lay out his mony to build or set forth Busses, and the Fisher-men be now so poore, by reason that they onely do beare the whole charge of that costly Hauen; the Merchant herring-buyers being not at any charge thereof, but all that great cost commeth out of the Fishermens labours, for the maintenance of that wodden Hauen, which amounteth to some fiue hundred pound a yeare, and some yeares more: so that though they be willing, yet there *Yermouth Hauen is the onely refuge, in distresse of whether, for all the Fishermen of the Cinque ports, and all other that doe fish in those seas, and it is built all of timber, against the violence of the maine sea: It is now in great danger to come to ruine, if they haue not help in time.*

ability

ability will not suffer them to do it, neither can they forbeare their mony for to aduenture their herrings into the East Countries where the best failes alwaies be.

To the North.wards of Yermonth eight leagues, are the Townes of Blakney and Wels, good Harbours and fit for Busses, and they haue good store of fishermen, and these townes haue some twenty Saile of Barkes, that they do ye rely send vnto Island; but these Townes be greatly decaied, to that they haue bene in the times passed, the which places, if that they had but 10. Busses belonging to them, would soone grow rich Townes in short time.

Then is there Lin a propper gallant Towne for Sea-faring men, and for men for Island; this is a rich Towne, and they haue some twenty Saile of Island ships, that they yearely send for Cods and Lings, and I am in hope to see them fall to the vse of Busses as soone as any men.

To the Northward is Boston, a propper Towne, and like vnto Holland soyle for low grounds and sands comming in, but yet there is but few Fishermen, but it is a most fit place for Busses, if that they had but once the taste of them they would soone finde good liking.

 Next to Boston some 20. leagues to the Northward, is the great riuer of Humber, wherein there is Hull, a very proper Towne of Saylors and Shipping, but there be but few fishermen but it is a most conuenient place for to aduenture Busses.

 There is also Grimsbey, Paul, and Pattrington: in all these places now there is great store of poore and idle people, that know not how to liue, and the most of all these places be decayed, and the best of them all grow worse and worse, which with the vse of Busses would soone grow rich Merchant-townes as is in Holland, for to these places would be transported out of the East-lands all manner of commodities, for the vse of Busses, and houses, and worke-yards erected for Coopers, and Rope-makers, & great numbers of Netmakers, and with the recourse of the Ships that shall bring salt and other commodities, & ships that shall lade away their Herrings and Fish, these places will soone become populous, and mony stirring plentifull in these places returned

for

for the procedue of fish and Herrings which places now bee exceeding poore and beggarly.

In all these fisher Townes that I haue before named, as *Colchester, Harwich, Orford, Alborough, Donwich, Walderswicke, Sowld, Yermouth, Blackney, wels, Lin, Boston,* and *Hul:* These be all the chiefest Townes, and all that vseth the North-seas in Summer and all these Townes it is well knowne be ruinated.

In all these Townes I know to be o--o Island Barkes, and o--o North-sea Boates, and all these Fishermen hauing o--o men a peece, amounteth to the summe of o--o. But admit that there is in all the West Country of England of Fisher-boats, tag and rag, that bringeth home all fresh fish, which seldome or neuer vseth any salt: say that they haue o--o men a peece, which make the summe of o--o in all England; but in all these I haue not reckoned the Fishermen, Mackrel-catchers, nor the Cobble-men of the North-country, which hauing o--o men a peece, commeth to so many men in all England.

I craue pardon, for that I omit the particular numbers and totall summe, which I could heere set downe, if I were commanded.

But so many in all England, and I haue truely shewed

And to imploy Ships and Marriners. 27

shewed before, that the Hollander hath in one Fleete of Busses twenty thousand Fishermen, besides all them that goeth in the Sword-pinks, Flat-bottomes, Carbskuits, Walnut-shels, and great Yeuers, wherein there is not lesse then 12000. more, and all these are onely for to catch Herrings in the North-seas.

Besides all them that goeth in the Flye-boates, for Shotland Lings, and the Pinks for barreld fish, and Trammell Boates, which commeth vnto 5000. more.

So that it is most true, that as they haue the summe of 0--0 Fishermen more then their is in all this Land: and by reason of there Busses, and Pinks, and Fishermen that set their Merchant Ships on worke, as that they haue 0--0 Fishermen more then we haue, so haue they 0--0 and 0--0 ships & Marriners more then we.

Now in our summe of 0--0 Fishermen, let vs see what vent haue we for our fish into other Countries, and what commodites and coine is brought into this Kingdome, and what Ships are set on worke by them, whereby Marriners are bred, or imployed, net one: It's pittifull.

D   For

For when our Fishermen commeth home, the first voyage from the North-seas, they goe either to London, Ipswich, Yermouth, Lin, Hull, or Scarbrough, and there they do sell at good rates, the first voyage, but the second voyage, because that they which be now the Fishermen haue not yet the right vse of making of barreld fish wherewith they might serue France, as doth the Hollanders, they be now constrained to sell in England, for that it is staple fish, and not being barreld the French will not buy it.

But if that our Fishermen had but once the vse of Pinks and Line-boats, and barreld fish, then they might serue France as well as the Hollanders, which by this new trade of Busses being once erected, and Pinks, and Line-boats, after the Holland manner, there will be Fishermen enow to manage the Pinks for barreld fish, from Nouember vnto the beginning of May, onely the most part of those men that shallbe maintained by the Busses, for that when the Busses do leaue worke, in the Winter their men shall haue employment, by the Pinks, for barreld fish, which men, now, do little or nothing,

And to imploy Ships and Marriners.

thing, for this laſt Winter at Yermouth, there was three hundreth Idle men that could get nothing to do, liuing very poore for lacke of imployment, which moſt gladly would haue gone to ſea in Pinks, if there had bene any for them to go in.

And whereas I before ſaid, that there was not one Ship ſet on work by our Fiſhermen, there may be obiected againſt me this.

That there doth euery yeare commonly lade at Yermouth 4. or 5. London Ships for the Streights, which is ſometimes true, & the Yermouth men themſelues do yearely ſend 2. or 3. Ships to *Bourdeaux*, and 2. or 3. Boates laden with herrings to *Roan*, or to *Nance*, or *S. Mallaus*, whereby there is returned, Salt, Wines, Normandy Canuice, whereby the King hath ſome cuſtome, but there is no mony returned into England for theſe Herrings, which coſt the Yermothians ready gold before that they had them of the Hollanders, and Frenchmen, to lade theſe Ships, and therefore I may boldly ſay not one.

No more Engliſh, but two ſmall Shippes, this yeare laded there.

And this laſt yeare, now, the Hollanders themſelues haue alſo gotten that trade, for there

F 2   did

Note heere how the Hollanders employ themselues and their Ships, first in taking of the herrings quick, and yet are not content but catch them againe after they bee dead, and doe set both their ships and Marriners on worke, and English ships ye vp a rotting.

did lade twelue Sailes of Holland Ships with red herrings at Yermouth, for *Ciuatauechia, Ligorne, Genoa,* and *Marsellis,* and *Talone,* most of them being laden by the English Merchants, so that if this be suffered, the English owners of Ships shall haue but small imployment for theirs.

Now to shew truely, what the whole charge of a Busse will be, with all her furniture, as Masts, Sailes, Ankors, Cables, and with all her Fishers implements, and appurtenances, at the first prouided all new, is a great charge, she being betweene 30. or 40. Last, will cost some fiue hundred pound.

By the Grace of God the Ship or Busse will continue twenty yeare with small cost and reparations, but the yearely slite and weare of her tackell, and war-ropes, and Nets will cost some eighty pounds.

And the whole charge for the keeping of her at Sea for the whole Summer, or three voiages, for the filling of a hundred Last of Caske, or Barrels.

100. Last

And to imploy Ships and Marriners. 31

100. Last of Barrels -- 72.	
For salt 4. months ----- 88.	
Beere 4. moneths ------ 42.	
For bread 4. months -- 21.	
Baken and Butter ----- 18.	
For pease 4. months -- 03.	
For billet 4. months --- 03.	
For mens wages 4. M. 88.	
335.	

A huudreth Last of Barrels, filled and sold at 10. pounds the Last commeth to one thousand pound.

Herrings 1000. li.
The whole charge 335.
gotten. 0665.

If any will know all the perticulars of weyes of Salt, or barrels of Beere, or hundreths of Biskets, I will willingly resolue them, but here is all the whole charge, and with the most.

Heere plainly appeareth that there is gotten 665. pounds in one Summer, whereout if that you do deduct one hundreth pounds for the weare of the Ship, and the reparations of her Nets against the next Summer, yet still there is 565. pounds remaining for cleare gaines, by one Busse, in one yeare. And I haue rated the herrings but at 10. pound the Last, which is with the least, for they bee commonly sold by the Hollanders at *Danske*, for 15. and 20. pounds the Last.

The Hollanders do make the profite of their Busses so certaine, that they do lay out their owne childrens mony, giuen them by their deceased friends in aduenturing in the Busses, and also there is in Holland a Treasury for Orphants, opened and layd out in aduenturing in the Busses.

The Hollanders do make both a profitable, and

F 3

and a pleasant Trade of this Summer fishing, for there was one of them, that hauing a gallant great new Busse of his owne, and he hauing a daughter married vnto one which was his Mate in the Busse, and the owner that was Maister of this Busse did take his wife with him aboord, and his Mate his wife, and so they did set saile for the North-seas, with the two women with them, the mother and the daughter, where hauing a faire wind, and being fishing in the North-seas, they had soone filled their Busse with herrings, and a Herring Yager commeth vnto them, and brings them gold and fresh supplies, and copeth with them, and taketh in their herrings for ready mony and deliuereth them more barrels and salt, and away goeth the Yager for the first Market into Sprucia, and still is the Busse fishing at sea, & soone after againe, was full laden, and boone home, but then another Yager commeth vnto him as did the former, & deliuering them more prouision of barrels and Salt, and ready mony and bid them fare-well, and still lyeth at Sea with the mother and daughter so long and not very long, before they had againe all their

Ready money or Tallyes, which are as bils of exchange to bee paid at first sight.

Barrels

Barrels full, and then they sailed home into Holland, with the two women, and the Busse laden with Herrings, and a thousand pounds of ready mony.

If that any man should make any question of the truth of this, it will be very credibly approued by diuerse of good credite that be now in the Citty of London.

Now to shew the charge of a pinke of eighteene or tweene Last, the Pinke being builded new, and all things new vnto her, will not cost two hundred and sixty pounds, with all her Lines, Hookes, and all her Fisher appurtenances.

 And 15. Last of Barrels will cost ———— 10.
   Fiue weyes of salt vpon salt ———— 15.
   For Beere and Caske ———— 07.
   For bread ———— 03.
   For butter ———— 01.
   For the Petty tally ———— 01.
For mens wages for 2 mo. M & all toge: — 20.
           57.

Fifteene last of barreld fish at 14. pound, and 8. shillings the Last, which is but 24. shillings the

the barrell amounteth vnto two hundreth and sixteene pounds, whereout if that you do deduct fifty and seuen pounds, for the charge of setting her to sea, their is still resting one hundreth fifty and eight pounds cleere gaines, by one Pinke, with fifteene Last of fish for two months.

Wherefore, seeing the profite so plainely, and by the grace of God so certaine, both by the Busses and Line-boates, whereby the Hollanders haue so long gained by, Let all Noble Worshipfull, and wealthy Subiects, put too their aduenturing and helping hands, for the speedy lanching, and floating forward of this great good Common-wealth businesse, for the strengthening of his Maiesties Dominions, with two principall pillars, which is, with plenty of coine brought in for fish, and herrings from other Nations, and also for the increasing of Marriners against all forraigne Inuasions, and also for the bettering of Trades and Occupations, and setting of thousands of poore and idle people on worke, which now know not how to liue, which by this Trade of the Busses shall be imployed, as daily we see is done before

And to imploy Ships and Marriners.

fore our eyes by the Hollanders. And as alwaies it hath bene seene, that those that be now the Fishermen of England, haue bene alwaies found to be sufficient to serue his Maiesties ships in former time, when their haue bene employment, which fellowes, by this new trade of building, and setting forth Busses will be greatly multiplyed and encreased in this Land; which fellowes, as we see the Hollanders, being well-fed in Fisher affaires, and strong and lustier then the Sailors that vse the long Southerne voyages, that sometimes are greatly surfeited, and hunger-pined But these couragious, yong, lusty, fed-strong yonkers, that shall qe bred in the Busses, when his Maiesty shall haue haue occasion for their seruice in warre, against the enemy, will be fellowes for the nonce, and will shew themselues right English, and will put more strength to an Iron Crow, at a peece of great Ordinance in trauersing of a Cannon, or Culuering, with the direction of the experimented Maister Gunner, then two or three of the fore named surfeited Sailors, and in distresse of winde growne sea, and fowle Winters weather, for flying forward word to their labour, for pulling in a topsaile, or a spret-saile, or shaking of a bonnet in a dark night, for wet and cold can not make them shrinke nor staine, that the North-seas, and the Busses, and Pinks haue dyed in graine, for such purposes.

And whosoeuer shall go to Sea, for Captaine to command in Marshall affaires, or take charge for Maister in trade of Merchandize, (as in times past I haue done both) will make choice of these fellowes, for I haue seene their resolution, in the face of their enemy, when they haue bene *legramenta*, and frolicke, and as forward as about their ordinary labours, or businesse.

It is not vnknowne, that this last yeare there was a generall presse along the Coast of England, frō Hull in Yorke-shire vnto S. Michaels Mount in Corne-wall, onely for Sailors, to furnish but 7. Shippes, for the wafting ouer of the Count Pallatine, and his most Noble Princes, but 28. leagues.

And when his Maiesty shall haue occasion and imployment for the furnishing of his Nauy there will be no want of Maisters, Pilots, Commanders, and sufficient directors of a course, and keeping of Computation, but now there is a pittifull want of sufficient good men to do the offices and labours before spoken of, all which, these men of the Busses and Pinks, will worthily supply.

And to the Art of Sayling they may hap-pily

And to imploy Ships and Marriners.

pily attaine, for hitherto it hath beene commonly seene, that those men, that haue beene brought vp, in their youth, in Fishery, haue deserued as well as any in the land for artificiall Sayling; for at this time is practised all the proiections of Circular and Mathematicall skales and Arithmeticall sayling, by diuers of the yong men of the Sea-coast Townes, euen as commonly amongst them as amongst the Theamsers.

Besides all the Hollanders before spoken of, the Frenchmen of Pickardy haue also a hundred Saile of Fishermen, onely for Herrings, on his Maiesties Seas euery yeare, in the Summer season, and they bee almost like vnto the Busses, but they haue not any Yagers that commeth vnto them, but they do lade themselues, and returne home twice euery yeare, and finde great profite by their making but of two voyages euery Summer season. *Some of these be 3. and 4. score Tunnes the burthen.*

And it is much to bee lamented, that wee hauing such a plentifull Countrey, and such store of able and idle people, that not one of his Maiesties Subiects, are there to be

Englands way to win wealth,

The Hollanders do yearely take so many, as they do make more then two millions of pound Sterling. And wee his Maiesties Subiects doe take no more then doe baite our hookes.

be seene all the whole Summer, to fish, or to take one Herring: But onely the North-sea boats of the Sea-coast Townes, that goeth to take Cods, they do take so many as they do need to baite their hookes and no more.

We are daily skorned by these Hollands, for being so negligent of our profite, and carelesse of our fishing, and they do daily floute vs that be the poore Fishermen of England, to our faces at Sea, calling to vs and saying, *Ya English, ya zall, or cud scoue dragien*, which in English is this: Yon English, we will make you glad for to weare our old shoes.

And likewise the French-men they say we are apish, for that we do still imitate them in all needlesse and fantasticall iagges and fashions, as it is most true indeed, for that they haue no fashion amongst them in apparell, nor Lace, Points, Gloues, Hilts, nor Garters, euen from the spangled Shoe-lachet, vnto the spangled Hat, and Hat-band, be it neuer so idle, and costly, but after that we do once get it, it is far bettered by our Nation.

Wherefore, seeing that we can excell all other Nations, wastfully, to spend mony, let

Vs

And to imploy Ships and Marriners.

Vs, in one thing, learne of other Nations, to get thousands out of his Maiesties Sea, and to make a generall profite of the benefites that Almighty God doth yearely send vnto vs, in far more greater aboundance then the fruite of our trees, which although they be more chargeable in the gathering together, yet is the profite far more greater, vnto this Kingdome, and Common wealth of all his Maiesties Subiects, increasing the wealth of the aduenturers; as also for the enriching of Merchants, and maintaining of Trades Occupations, and employing of Ships, and encreasing of Marriners, which now do but little or nothing: as also for the setting of poore and idle people on worke, which now know not how to liue, and to teach many a tall fellow to know the propper names of the ropes, in a ship, and to hale the bowline that now for lacke of employment many such, by the inconuenience of idle liuing, are compelled to end their daies, with a rope by an vntimely death, which by the employment of the Busses might be well auoyded, and they in time become right honest seruiceable and trusty Subiects.

The Sailors Prouerbe: The Sea and the Gallowes refuse none.

G 3   Here

Englands way to win wealth,

Here since my booke came to the Presse, I haue bene credibly certified, by * men of good worth (being Fishmongers) that since Christmas last, vnto this day, there hath bene paid to the Hollanders, here in London, onely for barreld fish, and Holland Lings, the summe of twelue thousand pound.

Mr. William nelling, M. tephen Topley, nd diuers others of the Company of ishmongers.

And last of all, if that there be any of the Worshipfull Aduenturers, that would haue any directions for the building of these Busses, or Fisher ships, because I know that the Shipcarpenters of England, be not yet skilfull in this matter, wherefore if that any shall bee pleased to repaire to me, I will bee willing to giue them directions, and plaine proiections, and Geometricall demonstrations for the right building of them, both for length, bredth, and depth, and also for their mould vnder water, and also for the contriuing of their roomes, and the laying of their geare, *according to the Hollanders fashion, any man shall heare of me at M. *Nathaniel Butters*, a Stationers Shop at Saint Austens gate in Paules Church-yard: Farewell this 18. of February.

And for prouiding of their Cordige, and Nets, after the most neatest & cheapest rates.

FINIS.

The States Proclamation, Translated out of Dutch.

The States generall of the United Prouinces of the low Countries vnto all those that shall see or heare these presents greeting, Wee let to weet that whereas it is well knowne, that the great fishing, and catching of herrings is the chiefest Trade, and principall Gold-mine of these United Countries, whereby many thousands of Housholds, Families, Handi-craftes, Trades and Occupations, are set on worke, well maintained, and prosper; especially the Sailing and Nauigation, as well within, as without these Countries, is kept in great esteemation: Moreouer many Returnes of Money, with the increase of the meanes, commerces, customes, and Renenues of these Countries are augmented thereby and prosper, and for asmuch as there is made from time to time many good Orders conseruing the catching, salting, and
beneficiall

beneficial vttering of the said Herrings, to the end to preserue and maintaine the said cheife Trade, in the United Prouinces; which Trade, by diuers encounters, of some that seeke their owne gaine, is enuied, in respect of the great good it bringeth to the United Conntries: and wee are informed that a new deuise is put in practise to the preiudice of the Trade, to transport out of the United Countries, into other Countries, Staues for herring-barrels made heere, and halfe herring barrels, put into other Barrels, and Nets: to crosse the good Orders and Pollicy here intended to them of these Conntres, for the catching, salting, and selling the herings, dressed in other Contries, after the order of these Countries, whereby this chiefe Trade should be decaied here, and the Inhabitants of these Countries damnified, if that we make not prouission, in time against such practises, therefore Wee, after Mature Iudgement, and Deliberation haue Forbidden and Interdicted, and by these Presents do forbid and interdict, all, and euery one, as well Home-borne and Inhabitants, as strangers frequenting these parts, to take vp any herring-barrels, or halfe ones prepared, or any kinde of Nets, in any Ship, Towne, or Hauen, of the vnited Prouinces, to be sent into other Countries, or Places, vpon paine of confiscation of the same, and the Ship also wherein they shall be found, besides a penalty ty of 200. of Netherlandish siluer Royals, for the first time, and for the second time aboue confiscation of Ship & Goods, & 400. of the said Royals of siluer, and for the third time, aboue confiscation of Ship and goods, and 600. of the said Royals of siluer, & corporal punishment: all which confiscations, and penalties, shall be distributed one third part to the profite of the Plantife, one third part to the poore, and one third part of the Officers, where the said confiscation shall be demanded: and not onely they shall incurre this penalty, which after shall be taken with the deed, but they also, that within one yeare after the deed shall bee conuicted, and that none may pretend ignorance, and that this order may be in all places duely obserued, and the offendors punished according to Iustice, Wee will and require, our deere and welbeloued Estates, Gouernours, Deputies of the councell, and the Estates of the respectiue Prouinces of Gilderland, and the county of Sacfill in Holland, West-Freesland, Zeland, Vtricts, Freesland, Merizel, the Towne of Groyning, and the circumiacent places, and to all Iustices and Officers, that they cause to bee published in all places, and proclaimed, where the vsuall Proclamation and Publication is made; We do charge also the chancellors, and Prouinciall councell, and the counsell of the Admiralty, the Aduocatisticall, and the Procurators generall, and all other Officers, Iudges,

H and

and Justices of these vnited Prouinces, and to all generall colonies, Admirals, and Vice-admirals, captaines, Officers, and commanders, to performe, and cause to be performed, this Order and commandement; and to proceed, and cause to be proceeded against the Offendors, without grace, fauour, dissimulation, or composition: because we haue found it necessary, for the good, and benefite, of the said United Prouinces, Dated in Hage this 19. of July.

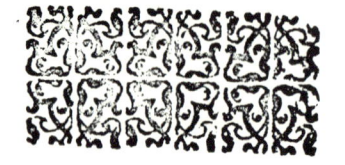

FINIS.

THE
TRADES
Increase.

LONDON,
Printed by *Nicholas Okes*, and are
to be sold by *Walter Burre.*
1615.

To the Reader.

Entle Reader, I commend vnto you a Polidorus his Treasure; yet without either murther or theft, but else as rich. So I confesse without leaue, neither may the Authour bee offended, if what I haue borrowed for my priuate vse, I haue payed to the seruice of the Common-wealth, in that what hee intended at the instance of one, being written, is behouefull o euery one.

One Pithius, a crafty Sicilian, finding an honest Romane Gentleman, called Canius, Desirous of a pleasant Garden in the Iland, he inuited him to his, and conducted diuers poore Fishermen to attend that day his Bankes, with Boates and Nets; and to bring in plenty of fish, and to lay them at his feete. The Guest asking what that meant, was answered by the Huxter, That it was the Royalty of that place, there was more fish thereabouts, then in any other streame of Syracuse And as oft as he repaired thither, that seruice was due, and done vnto him. The poore Gentleman was taken with the Nets, and presently dealeth with the owner for the Garden, who suffering himselfe to be much improtuned, at the length was intreated to sell it full deerely: The day following, the buyer, disposed

To the Reader.

sed to shew the magnificence of his purchase, inuiteth diuers friends to accompany him thither, and missing the concourse and confluence of his expected homagers, the Fishermen (For there was neither Boate, Oare, Net, or Fin of fish to be seene) *asketh his new neighbours whether it were a holiday for Fishermen? The plaine folk answered,* None they knew of; *& further wondred at the former resort, for they neuer saw before Boates or Fishermen there. In a word, hee was cosened. But it is not so in this fishing Proiect, to the which you are now inuited frankely and plainely;* Nullæ hic piscatorum feræ; *we may alwaies fish here without feare of any* Sicilian *purchase, or scarcity of the Romane* Macrobius *his Table, where there was* Piscis, *but* paucorū hominum. *Here is fish, the King of fish, the meate and Marchandize of both remote and neighbour Nations. To perswade hereto, the Authour hath dealt by way of comparison, not thereby to derogate from other* Trades, *but to aduance this Mysterie, and indeed, to shew that they may all receiue true nourishment from this nursery. Let therefore no man take that with the left hand which is offered with the right. And though, by the opinion of some of vnderstanding in those faculties, there is a reasonable suruey giuen of our* Sea-trades, State, *and* Breeding; *and out of others iudgements, there is euen* Candor animi *in all particulars, without either suspicion of any personall taxation offered, or any States blot suspected: Yet I desire also to professe the Authours true and faire meaning herein, and to make good the ouersights that may bee committed in the particular trauerse, with that of the Poet,* Vbi plurima nitent, Non ego

To the Reader.

ego paucis offendor maculis. Of the ſubiect it ſelfe I will onely ſay thus much, That if Aurum portans hath beene alwaies welcome, hence you may receiue gold, pay the Kings duties, and doe your Countrey ſeruice; and ſo I leaue theſe buſineſſes to their own abilities, and take my leaue of you with this concluſion of them.

Niſi peracta luduntur.

L. R.

The Trades Increase.

SEEING by chance a late Treatise entitled, *Englands way to winne wealth, &c.* and being easily inuited to reade the same, euen for the Titles sake; I must confesse my selfe so affected with the proiect, that I presently resolued to goe a fishing, withall concluding with my selfe, that as there is no fishing to the sea: so there was no fish in the sea like to the Herring: and for that my estate is but meane, and my selfe a fresh-water Souldier, it requireth cost, and I would haue company: the sea is large enough, and hath roome enough for vs all, and there are Herrings enough to make vs all rich: for that I say a man may runne a course this way to enrich himselfe, to strengthen his countrey, to enable his Prince more honestly then many late sea-courses can warrant vs in, more easily, more safely, more certainly then any other

B sea-

sea-courſe can perſwade vs to whatſoeuer; I could not chooſe, out of my allegeance to my Prince, out of my duety to my Countrey, out of my loue to my neighbour, but commend theſe motiues concerning the ſame to a further conſideration, conſiſting,

In the { Neceſſitie, Facilitie, Profit, and Vſe of } fiſhing.

The neceſſity out of want of { Shipping. Mariners. Imploiment of mē.

As concerning ſhips, it is that which euery one knoweth, and can ſay, they are our weapons, they are our ornaments, they are our ſtrength, they are our pleaſures, they are our defence, they are our profit; the ſubiect by them is made rich, the kingdome through them ſtrong, the Prince in them mighty; in a word, by them in a manner we liue, the kingdome is, the king reigneth. If the ſea faile, the *Venetians* they fall; and if we want ſhips, wee are diſſolued. *Eſops* Sheepheard kept his flocke well ſo long as he nouriſhed his dogge; but when the Wolfe had perſwaded him that he was ſuperfluous, hee coſened him eaſily of all his ſheepe. It is the kingdomes caſe in ſhipping, which made that heroicall King of *Denmarke* at his view of the Kings maieſties Nauy at *Chattam*, confeſſe he then ſaw the ſtrength of *England*, the greatneſſe of our

King,

King, *In sola tanta est fiducia Naue.*

Concerning the want of shipping, though to suppresse the consideration thereof be very material, yet the poynt it selfe is to be handled very tenderly: for that as I haue no pleasure to touch our owne wounds, so I am loath in this case to discouer our owne wants; for that I feare the enemie will sooner take the aduantage of them, then wee will be stirred vp thereby to make supply. To giue therefore the true and faithfull subiect a darke Lanthorne whereby hee may onely see himselfe, and he not be seene, setting the contemplation of the Kings royall Nauy aside, so mighty, so well conditioned, which hath so many good Officers, and such worthy Ouer-seers, which is so chargeable to his Maiestie to maintaine, as I hope it will neuer be safe for the enemy to meddle withall: setting, I say, this aside, our Merchants Nauie consisteth in the Shippes

Want of shipping.

For
- The Straights.
- Spaine.
- France.
- Hambrough and Middlebrough.
- The Sound.
- Newcastle.
- Island.
- New found Land.
- The East Indies.

I haue not named *Moscouie*, because we haue in a manner lost that Trade, the troubles of that king-

kingdome, and our desire of security hauing depriued vs therof, which we may the more lament, becaufe I haue heard Marchants affirme, that in these vncomfortable daies of aduenturing, it was one of their best Trades, and with no small meruaile yet vpheld, and most prouidently followed by the Hollanders, we being scarred away from so good & profitable a trade, as birds from Cherrie-trees, with the shew of dead carkasses, or shout of boyes, whilst other lusty and plumpe laddes haue wililie beate away the children, beate downe the scarre crowes, and stolen the fruite away, to their great gaine, and our disgrace, there repairing not thither aboue two Ships English in stead of seuenteene of great burden for the company formerly, besides Enterlopers, to the great decay of our Marchants and shipping: whereas the Hollander (according to a credible report made) betweene the Ward-house and the East-ward, at *Tippenie, Kilden, Olena,* and the Riuer *Cole* at *Colmograue*, and at Saint *Nicholas* in *Russia*, had aboue thirty fiue sailes of their Shippes the last yeare. Happily some will say, that they made so poore a voyage that they had bene better kept themselues at home; and it is very likely, yet the yeare before, they had some thirty saile, and now this yeare they haue againe repaired their Nauy, renewed their aduenture, and sent neere as many, as neither dismaied with troubles, nor yet discouraged with losse; and to make it the more strange that they shold thus preuet our trade, & increase their own: as it was after vs that they came thither euen by

The Countrey being afflicted with war, and the Hollanders will, petere cibum è flamma.

leaue

leaue, as it were, to gleane with our Reapers, (for the fields were ours) the difcouery of the Land, and Trade wholy ours, found out by *Chanceler* and *Willoughby*, and euer fince continued by our Merchants) fo againe their beft Trade thither, is maintained euen by our owne commodities, as Tinne, Lead, Courfe-clothes and Kerfeis: the inconuenience whereof, together with the preuention, I leaue to the fenfible confideration, to the fufficient ability of the *Mofcouie* Marchant, who I feare can fcarce heare mee, being (as I faid) gone fo farre as the *Eaſt-Indies*; and if I fhould fend to him, I feare I fhould not finde him at leafure, hauing thither tranfported much of the *Mofcouie* Staple. For the Marchants that formerly vfed the *Mofcouie* Trade are now there feated; and becaufe as we know it is warmer there, and as they find it, it is very profitable, we will alfo by Compaffe trauell thither our felues; that as *Valeria* a faire Lady, anfwering to *Scilla* in the Theater, being demanded, Why fhee preffed fo neere, faid; That thereby fhee might haue fome of his felicity; fo by being in their company, wee may communicate with them of their good fortunes, or commune with them of our wants.

Primo Edw.6.

So then, to beginne our iourney at the nobleft place for worth, and one of the neweft in knowledge, the worthieft in former remembrance, the worft in prefent reputation, for the bottome of the *Straights*, the firft in name, and whilome a very materiall bufines of Marchandize: I do find this Trade but eafie, and the difficulties many and new

The Straights.

new, the Trade it selfe being lessened by the circumuention of the *East-Indie* nauigation, which fetcheth the Spices from the well head; and I find the rest of the benefites alayed, by charges, by insultation of Pirates, and infidelity of seruants. These make presents and profit of their Maisters goods abroad, so farre, that some of the owners become lame at home: Pirates meete with that whereby others are extreamly hindred, and by the charges the rest are exceedingly discouraged, so that the Merchants returne is but poore, and the nauigation much lessened, the employment thitherward fayling in neere thirty shippes, & those of such burden, that they were of defence and renowne to the kingdome. I heard a worthy Marchant in his time *Thomas Cordell* of *London* say, that on the first beginning of the *Turkey* Trade, his selfe with other Merchants, hauing occasion to attend the late Queens Maiesties Priuy Councell about that businesse, they had great thanks & commendations for the shippes they then builded of so great a burden for those partes, by the Earles of *Bedford* and *Leicester*, and other honorable Personages, with many encouragements to goe forward (euen to vse their owne words) for the *Kingdomes sake*, notwithstanding it was then to their great benefite likewise, whose ordinarie returnes at the first were three for one, which I speake not out of enuy. For as all callings are, and ought to be maintained through the profite that ariseth thereby, labours rewarded, dangers recompenced by the sweat and sweet of gaine; nay,

I in

in our moſt Liberall Profeſſions, the Diuine for his ſpirituall nouriſhment hath temporall foode; the Phyſition for the care of the body asketh the comfort of the purſe; and the Lawyer muſt bee payd for his Plea: ſo Merchants of all Companies the moſt liberall, are likewiſe of all ſortes the moſt worthie to gaine, *Vt qui per vniuerſum orbem diſcurrunt, mare circumluſtrantes & aridam;* to vſe that hopefull Prince in his time King *Edward* the ſixt his words in a Letter to forren Princes, in Sir *Hugh Willoughbie* his behalfe. But to end my long Parentheſis, I ſpeake it I ſay out of pitty, to ſee now the returne ſo meane, the Merchant ſo diſcouraged, the ſhipping ſo diminiſhed: and to conclude this poynt without loue or anger, but with admiration of our neighbours the now *Sea-herrs*, the Nation that get health out of their owne ſickeneſſe, whoſe troubles begot their liberty, brought foorth their wealth, and brought vp their ſtrength, that haue out of our leauings gotten themſelues a liuing, out of our wants make their owne ſupply of Trade and ſhipping there; they comming in long after vs, equall vs in thoſe partes in all reſpects of priuilege and port; that haue deuanced vs ſo farre in ſhipping, that the *Hollanders* haue more then one hundred ſaile of ſhippes that vſe thoſe parts, continually going and returning, and the chiefeſt matters they doe lade outward, be *Engliſh* Commodities, as Tinne, Lead, and Bailes of ſuch like ſtuffe as are made at *Norwich*.

 For the reſt of the Straights, one ſide, as the coaſt

Beeing bound for diſcoueries Prim.Ed.6.

See-herren.

coast of *Barbary*, serues onely for places and Cities of refuge, not after the Diuine *Leuiticall* law, when one hath killed a man by chance there to be succoured: but after that diabolicall *Alcoran*, when any haue robbed and murdered abroad, thither they may repaire, be in safety, and enioy.

 The other side, as *Naples, Genoa, Ligorne*, and *Marseilles*, employ some twenty saile, and they most with Herring. For the Ports neere to the Straights mouth, as *Malega*, &c. wee haue some store of shipping, as about thirtie saile, that begin in Iune to set forth some for *Ireland*, to lade Pipe-staues in their way to *Malega*, they returning *Malega* wines. But the *Hollanders* likewise haue found out that Trade, and be as busie amongst the Irish as our selues for Pipe-staues: nay, by your leaue, they haue beene too busie there of late with some of our poore Country-mens wind-pipes; but that is besides the matter heere. But for *Malega* it selfe, the Inhabitants there haue through our plentifull resort thither, planted more store of Vines, so that on our recourse thither, our marchants haue withdrawne themselues much from *Cherris*.

Spaine.

 For *Andalusia, Quantado, Lisberne, Portugall*, it is easily knowne what shipping wee haue there by our Trade, which is but meane, consisting in Sacke, Sugar, Fruit, and *west-Indie* Drugs, which may employ some twenty ships. Amongst these *Cherris* Sackes are likewise brought into *England*, especially in *Flemish* Bottomes.

 For the bringing in from thence any store of salt by vs, it is excepted against, we being by report furnished

furnished principally by the *Hollanders* of most of the salt that our Fisher Townes do vse for the salting of Island fish, and all other Fish for Herring and Staple-fish, as the Ports of *London, Colchester, Ipswich, Yarmouth, Linne, Hull, Scarbrough*, can testifie. *Albrough* men were wont to bring it in, especially employing some thirty or forty Saile belonging to it, of some seuen or eight score, or two hundred Tunne; which for the most part, were set on worke all the yeare long, with transporting of coales from *Newcastle* to *France*, and fetching salt from thence; which Trade is now much decayed with *France*, by the double dilligence of the *Hollanders*, who serue vs principally from *Spaine*.

For our Trade to *Burdeaux*, it is lightly as great *France*. as euer it was: For I do not thinke there was euer more Wine drunke in the Land. Yet that voyage appeareth not to be so beneficiall in regard of the small rate that the Owners and Sea-men haue thither-ward. *France* may euery way employ, and those most small vessels, some threescore ships and barkes.

To *Hambrough* and *Middlebrough* there are be- *Hambrough &* longing six or seuen ships to each place, and they *Midalebrough,* lade for the Company (and are called *Appointed Ships*) euery three months in all the yeare, there may be laden some thirty odde Shippes, and they but 14 or 15 bodily. But as they make, as is said, two voyages the Ship, how it standeth with them, or how they will stand, it is vncertaine in regard of the manner of the altering of Trading with their cloath. Once for certaine the Merchant aduenturers

C

shipping and Mariners. I doubt me whether if they had such a treasure, they would not imploy their owne shipping. The *French* saile hither in whole Fleetes, some forty or fifty saile together, especially in Summer, seruing all their Portes of *Picardie*, *Normandie*, and *Brittaine*, euen as farre as *Rochel* and *Bourdeaux*, with their owne shippes and sailers from *Newcastle*. So they of *Breame*, *Embden*, *Holland* and *Zealand* do serue all *Flaunders*, and the Archdukes Countries, whose shipping is not great: These paying no more then his Maiesties owne naturall subiects, if they transport any coales. Which imposition, say our men, made our Countrey men forbeare their carrying any more Coales abroad, because the *Frenchmen* would not giue aboue their old rate: and which was worse, thereby they sold away their shippes, some to *France*, some to *Spaine*, some to other Countries. Whereby sure their faults are more apparant then their ill fortune, in that though their gaine was lesse at the instant, by the imposition then formerly; yet to leaue the Trade, argued neither good spirits, nor great vnderstanding, nor any especiall good minde to their Countrey. For whence I pray you came such a necessity to leaue the Trade and to giue ouer shipping, as if they could not liue thereby; when presently forraigne Nations fell to the Trade themselues, as is formerly set downe, and fetch away our coales on the same tearmes which wee do refuse? And by report, notwithstanding the fiue shillings imposed, the *French* do sell in *France* one Chauldron of coales aduenturers ſhips haue been alwaies formerly the ſure ſtay of Merchants ſeruices both for their readineſſe, goodneſſe, and number of ſhipping touching the common-wealths affaires.

The Sound.   For *Danske, Melvin* and *Quinsbrough*, there are not aboue fiue or ſixe ſhippes of *London*, that vſe thoſe places, as many more of *Ipſwich*, and ſo likewiſe from *Hull, Linne*, and *Newcaſtle*, the like proportion reſorteth thither for Trade. Theſe make ſome two returnes in the yeare: but in all thoſe places the *Hollanders* doe abound, and bring in more commodities by fiue times to vs, then our owne ſhipping. And for *Liefland*, the *Narue, Rye,* and *Reuell*, the *Hollanders* haue all the Trade in a manner; the commodities from theſe former places being Corne, Flaxe, Sope-aſhes, Hempe, Iron, Waxe, and all ſorts of Deale.

For *Norway* we haue not aboue fiue; and they aboue forty ſaile, and thoſe double or treble our burden euen for the Citty.

Newcaſtle.   The next is *Newcaſtle* Trade, and for certaine the chiefeſt now in *eſſe*, for maintenance of ſhipping, for ſetting Sea-fearing men on worke, and for breeding daily more, there may be about ſome two hundred ſaile of *Caruiles*, that onely vſe to ſerue the Citty of *London*, beſides ſome two hundred more that ſerue the ſea-coaſt towns throughout *England*, ſmall and great, as Barques and other ſhipping of ſmaller burden, and more might eaſily be: for hither euen to the Mines mouth, come all our Neighbour Country Nations with their Shippes continually, employing their owne
ſhipping

for as much money as will buy three or foure of *Newcastle*. Had they held to with patience, either they might haue brought the stranger to their price, or else by due order and discreet fashion opened the inconueniency to the state, of the strangers stomack in refusing their Coale, and fetching them their selues: so as they might easily haue wearied them, and won their Trade and gaine againe; whereas now they are beggard, our Country disfurnisht of shipping. The stranger keeping his coine at home, bringeth hither bare and base commodities, their shipping & Mariners are employed and increased; and notwithstanding the *Argus* eyes of the Searcher, carry gold away with them, alwaies bringing more in stocke with them, then they carry away in commodities.

For to make a motion to haue this fiue shillings excused in our owne Nation, is rather profitable then necessary, in regard wee see the stranger thriueth notwithstanding it, and it being done out of his Maiesties royal prerogatiue, *& ex causa lucratiua*, as is apparant by what the stranger gaineth; and the like is willingly imbraced here in other transportations, as Beere, &c. were, me thinkes, vndutifull likewise. But to mention a motion very lately made, and generally amongst his Maiesties loyall subiects imbraced; Might it please his Maiesty to make and ordaine a Staple Towne in *England* for Sea-coale, and we haue many fit places, and Harbours more neere and proper then that of *Tinmouth*, at *Newcastle* (and herein as I am bound in affection to wish well to *London*, so I must, out of of many mens iudgements, commend *Harewich*, *statio bene fida Carinis*, and then lying fit for the Low-countries, and indeed open to all Nations by the benefite of the large sea which washeth it) whereby strangers shall be restrained from further Trade to *Newcastle*, and shall all repaire to the said Staple Towne to fetch their Coales: Besides that it would be an exceeding benefite to his Maiesty, it would likewise helpe vs in this our complaint of want of shipping. For by this meanes our *English* bottomes bringing all the Coales to the Staple Towne, shall not onely be set on worke, but increase will follow in Shipping. The *Venetians* sometime passed being out-gone by those of *Zant* in their custome, drew the Trade from the Grecians, and planted as it were, a Colonie of Curranes at *Venice*. If for a little custome, and to pull downe their suspected subiects swelling mindes, they did so, why should not his Maiesty for the increase of his Shipping, and the releiuing of the prostrate estate of his faithfull and humble subiects, take this warrantable course?

Island voiage entertaineth 120 ships and barkes. *Island.*
New found Land employeth some 150 saile, from all parts, of small ships, but with great hazard; and therefore that voyage, feared to be spoiled by heathen and sauage, as also by Pirates. *New found Land*

Now followeth the consideration of the East Indie Trade, into whose seas, not onely the Riuer of *Volga*, as before you heard, disemboqueth it self, but euen the bottome of the *Straights* is emptied to fill vp those gulfes, and not so onely, but besides that *East Indies.*

that many of our best Marchants haue transported their Staples thither; it hath also begot out of all Callings, Professions, and Trades, many more new Merchants. Then where there is increase of Merchants, there is increase of Trade; where Trade increaseth, there is increase of Shipping; where increase of Shipping, there increase of Mariners likewise: so then rich and large *East Indies*. The report that went of the pleasing notes of the Swannes in *Meander* floud, farre surpassing the records of any other birds in any other places whatsoeuer, drew thither all sorts of people in great confluence, and with great expectation to heare, and enioy their sweete singing. When they came thither, they found in stead of faire white Swans, greedy Rauens, and deuouring Crowes; and heard, in stead of melodious harmony, vntuneable and loathsome croaking. In indignation that they were so receiued and deceiued, in stead of applauding, they hissed; and of staying, fled away. You are now braue *East Indies*, *Meander* floud, your Trade is the singing of Swannes, which so many iourney so farre to enioy. God forbid you should be found so discoloured, and we so ill satisfied. And howsoeuer that I may be sure to auoide any detraction, whereby my nature might haue any imputation, or by calling vp more spirits into the circle then I can put downe againe, I might incurre some danger, and be taxed likewise of indiscretion, for that we onely hitherto haue complained of the want of Shipping; we desire now but herein to suruey the store, and see how

you

you helpe the increase. You haue built more Ships in your time, and greater farre then any other Merchants Ships; besides what you haue bought out of other Trades, and all those wholly belonging to you; there hath beene entertained by you since you first aduentured, one and twentie Ships, besides the now intended voiage of one new Ship of seuen hundred Tunne; and happily some two more of increase. The least of all your Shipping is of foure score Tunne: all the rest are goodly Shippes, of such burthen as neuer were formerly vsed in Merchandize; the least and meanest of these last is of some hundred and twentie Tunne, and so go vpward euen to eleuen hundred Tunne. You haue set forth some thirteen voyages, in which time you haue built of these, eight new Shippes, and almost as good as built the most of the residue, as the *Dragon*, the *Hector*, &c. so that at the first appearance you haue added both strength and glory to the Kingdome by this your accession to the Nauy. But where I pray you are all these Ships? foure of these are cast away, of the which one was of three hundred Tunne, another of foure hundred, the third of three hundred, and the fourth of eleuen hundred; two more are docked vp there as Pinaces to Trade vp and down: the rest are either employed in the Trade in the *Indies*, or at home out of reparations; which if true, if the Kingdome should haue need of them on any occasion, it shall surely want their seruice; and so then there is not onely no supply to the Nauy this way, but hurt euen to the whole kingdome, the woods
being

being cut downe, and the Shippes either loft, or not ſeruiceable. Surely ſtories can ſhew vs, which we may reade in the courſes of Common-weales, how tolerable, nay how laudable it is in all States, to enlarge Commerce. Merchants whom wee ſhould reſpect, can tell vs of the caſualties which not onely the Ships, but their eſtates are ſubiect to by aduentures. Mariners whom we muſt pitty, can teach vs of the ordinary dangers not onely that Shippes and goods, but their liues are ſubiect to by ſea. I muſt not then exprobrate that to them which is to be imputed to the Sea; nor are they to be blamed out of reaſon for that which deſerueth, in humanity, commiſeration; nor is *England* bounded by our Horizon, to go no further then we ſee. We haue learned long ſince, that *Mercatura ſi tenuis ſordida, ſi magna ſplendida:* the ſtranger the Country, the greater the aduenture; the more famous our Nation, the more worthy the Merchant. Before wee were, euen *Horace* writ, *Currit Mercator ad Indos.* Loath then am I to borrow that ſaying of *Demoſthenes* on his courting of *Lais*, to pay it to the *Indian* Trade, by alleaging, that *Non tanti Emam pœnitentiam*, only hauing now in common that *Roman proutſo, Ne quid detrimenti reſp. capiat.* Let vs examine that which may moue patience, that our woods are cut downe, and the Ships either loſt or not ſeruiceable: Our woods I ſay, cut downe in extraordinary manner, neither do the Shippes die the ordinary death of Shippes. Our woods extraordinarily cut downe, in regard of the greatneſſe of the Shipping, which

doth

doth as it were deuoure our timber. I am able out of sufficient testimony to affirme, that since the *Indian* Trade, and meerely through their building of their ships of so great burthen, and their repairing (the building notwithstanding beganne but fiue yeares since) that timber is raised in the Land fiue shillings, and more, in the loade, nay, almost not to be had for money, which the Company (no question) being sensible of, very wisely seeke to helpe themselues in, by building of ships in *Ireland* for their seruice: yet it seemeth their incouragement that was, is but *necessitous* in regard by their owne saying besides the hazard, the charges are little lesse; and which is worse, that kinde of timber is but vntoward for that vse, being so extreame heauy, that a ship of small burden, draweth much water. If in fiue yeares space their building, together with their repairing of shippes, almost equall to building, beget such a scarcitie, what will a little continuance bring forth? Bring forth I cannot say ought, but a priuation will follow euen of all our timber-wood. The Kings Nauy must be maintained, other Marchants of lower ranke must haue shipping, and the sea-trade may increase, and then either wee must trade without shipping, or make ships without timber.

When the *Norman Conquerour* hauing subdued the most part of the kingdome, passed from *Essex* into *Kent*, which then made head against him, the *Kents*, hauing by the aduice of their politique Bishop, and their stout Abbot, cut downe great boughes, and with them in their armes marched

D towards

towards the *Conquerour*; whereby, besides the nouelty of the sight, the Army appeared double as big. *William* himselfe so conceiuing it, as also amazed to see woods walke; more feared and discontented with that sight, then otherwise assured with his former successe, condescended to what demands soeuer were made by those people, to haue such weapons laid downe, and to gaine such ingenious subiects; whereby, to their eternall benefite, and credite, their persons were neuer in bondage, nor their Lawes altered. In this their Land-stratageme, I see our sea-Arts, in that and these woods being the fatal instrument of our fortunes, boughes of Trees kept the *Kentish-men* out of seruitude, when they held them in their hands, and but for shew; their bodies will keepe vs in liberty when they containe vs, and are for seruice, and by their mouing on the water they will amaze both *French* and *Spanish*, and whomsoeuer, and keepe them, and all others, from comming neere vs: Out of which prouident fore-sight, our most worthy Princes formerly raigning, haue made diuers Lawes in fauour of timber trees: and our most noble King hath prouided therto with new accessions for the preseruing and increasing of them; but that a parricide of woods should thus be committed by building of ships, it was neuer thought on by any of our royall *Solons*, and therefore there was no prouiso for it: Nay, this inconuenience was so little suspected, that our sayd famous Princes haue prouided cleane contrary, with great bounty and indulgence, hauing encoraged

34. Hen. 8. 17.
13. Eliz. 25.

Forbidding by Proclamation the building with Timber.

raged by reward out of their owne purses the builders of great ships; as bestowing on the builders fiue shillings on the Tun for euery Tunne that is builded aboue one hundred Tun in a ship, so necessary did the Prince thinke his maintenance of shipping, the accession thereof consisting much in their greatnesse, to the honour and safety of the Kingdome;& such vse he made account he should haue of them. Whereas now this way he contributeth, to the spoile of his woods, to the losse of the ships, and to the hurt of the Kingdome. I heard a Ship-wright say on the losse of the *Trades Increase*, that if you ride forty miles from about *London*, you could not finde sufficient Timber to build such an other. It was a ship of eleuen hundred Tunne: for beauty, burthen, strength, and sufficiency, surpassing all Marchants ships whatsoeuer. But alas! shee was but shewne, out of a cruell destiny shee was ouertaken with an vntimely death in her youth and strength; being deuoured by those Iron wormes of that Country, that pierced her heart, and brake many a mans withall memorable in her misfortune, onely redounding to the Commonwealthes losse. For as for the Marchants, though I pitie their aduentures with all my heart, yet in this their part of losse was least; for all their goods were on shore; and she had brought aboundance out of the *Mecha* Fleete, which she did both tith and toll: And thankes be to God, they are more then sauers by what is returned from her, and more then that often, by the grace of God, will come from her to the Marchants gaine.

D 2 The

The like vntimely fall had the other three of great burthen, gallant ships, neuer hauing had the fortune to see their natiue soile againe, or the honour to do their Country any seruice, in respect of all other ships that wander ordinarily to other Countries, therefore I may iustly say that they die not the ordinary death of ships, who commonly haue some rest, and after long seruice die full of yeares, and at home, much of their timber seruing againe to the same vse, besides their Iron-worke, and the rest otherwise seruiceable, and not in this bloudy and vnseasonable fashion, rather indeed as coffins full of liue bodies, then otherwise as comfortable shippes. For the rest that liue, they come home so crazed and broken, so maimed and vnmanned, that whereas they went out strong, they returne most feeble: and whereas they were carried forth with Christians, they are brought home with Heathen. What the profits are to the Marchants, for so great an aduēture, I know not. I am sure amends cannot easly be made for so great a losse, euen in this point which is our special subiect now, for wast of woods, & spoile of shipping.

Our ships are faine to take in the natiues of the Indian Countries to supply the wants of our dead Sea-men to bring home their shippes.

And thus we haue surueyed all the fountaines whence our shipping especially doth flow: which before I shut vp, I remember me of a new Spring in *Greeneland*, that batheth some ships and burdeneth them likewise with her owne natural fraight, with the which the Whale is so richly loaden withall. This place is but of late frequented so especially, and hath employed this last yeare some foureteene ships, and more would do, but that the

poore

poore Fishermen, who though they knew the place before, yet being belike afraid of the Whale, are now swallowed vp in the Whales ships.

The Moscouy Merchants haue procured an inhibition for all others from fishing there.

I cannot finde any other worthy place of forren anchorage. For the *Bermudas*, we know not yet what they will doe; and for *Virginia* we know not well what to do with it: the present profit of those not employing any store of shipping: and for this other it is yet but *Embrion:* no question a worthy enterprise and of great consequence, much aboue the Marchants leuell & reach. And sure in regard of the great expences they haue beene at, and the poore returne that is made, they are much to bee regarded & commended for holding out so long: I could wish, that as many of the Nobility and Gentry of the land haue willingly embarqued themselues in the labour, so the rest of the Subiects might be vrged to help to forme and bring forth this birth, not of an infant, but of a man; nay, of a people, of a kingdom, wherein are many kingdomes. When *Alcmena* was in trauell with *Hercules*, the Poets say *Iupiter* was faine to be Midwife; and sure, as we haue the countenance of our earthly *Iupiter*, so we are humbly to emplore the propitious presence of our heauenly God, toward the perfection of this so great a worke. And so leauing to medle further with what we haue nothing to do, let vs returne to our ships, out of whose entertainements we may either reioyce at their increase, or by other obseruations preuent their decay: & because we propounded to our selues the necessity of our home-fishing out of the want of

D 3   our

our shipping, we will affirme that by this our superficiall view we find a decay thereof, & that out of two reasons; because that in places formerly frequented, our shipping lesseneth, and in places new found, they doe not succeed: we haue giuen reasonable probability of these already without any pleasure, & there is no need of repetition, and it will be more apparant in the preferring of this desire of Fishing, out of the examination of the next inducem̅ēt therto, which is *want of Mariners*.

<small>Want of Mariners.</small>

Mariners, they vse the weapons, shippes, they weare the ornaments, shippes, out of them ships, are strength and pleasure: otherwise they are but Pictures, that haue but a shew, or are as carkasses bereft of life. It is the good Pilot that bringeth the Shippe to the Hauen: It is the wise Maister that gouerneth the men in the Ship; but without men the Maister cannot gouerne, nor the shippe goe: What is a Leader without an Army, and that of Souldiers? the same reason of Sea-men in a ship; the body must haue life, bloud and flesh: the same are Sea-men to a shippe. *Columbus* found out the new world, *Drake* brought home the hidden treasure in a ship; but they were both prouided well of men, and gouerned well: therefore as Shippes are manned; and as Masters vse their men, so ordinarily their shippes succeede. As for this last matter of gouernement, it is besides our busines, wee will leaue that to whom it concerneth. Now then, though wee cannot vse shipping without men, and therefore they must goe together; yet we must consider the one after the other, and hauing

uing looked into the ſtrength of the one, we will view in them the ſtate of the other, in the which wee will not be long, for that the ſubiect is vnpleaſant, and our Tale is halfe tolde already: for the conſequence is neceſſary. As ſhippes are employed, ſo men are buſied.

For *Moſcouy*, it is apparant that the ſhipping thitherward is decayed; ſo neither Mariners are well employed that way, nor any Sea-men almoſt bred. The fleete that went ordinarily thitherward entertained three or foure Nouices in a ſhip, and ſo bred them vp Sea-men, which might make in the whole happily ſome foure ſcore men yearely, which was well for their partes. Now then there were ſome fiue hundred Mariners and Saylers employed withall: ſo then this way there is want.

The like reaſon of the Straights in their proportion, the very bottome of the Straights failing in thirtie ſhippes, maketh yearely ſeuen hundred Sea-men and Mariners at the leaſt, ſeeke ſome other courſes which were that way employed, beſides the vnder-growth hindred of ſome hundred and forty ſea-men yearly. And but that I am loath to renue our complaints; I would ſay it were great pitty of this ſo great an ebbe of our men in theſe ſeas, for that beſides the voyages were of encouragement euen to the *Frie*, all in generall commonly went and returned in good health, a ſhip ſeldome looſing a man in a voyage; nay, I heard a proper Maiſter of a ſhippe ſay, that in eighteene yeares, wherein he frequented thoſe parts, he loſt

not

not two men out of his ship: and whatsoeuer may bee imputed to the incontinencie of our men, or the vnwholsomnesse of the women in other places, surely in those parts I heare the common sort of women to be as dangerous, and the generalitie of our men as idely disposed.

Naples, Ligorne, Marseilles, and those parts of the straights, may imploy some foure hundred men, and breed of these about forty.

Malega imploying besides some foure hundred men, the imployment that may come by all other places in *Spaine* and *Portugall*, not arriuing to foure hundred men, in regard of the pouerty of the trade, and the superfluity of the commodities, it being indeede rather entertained because they will not be idle, otherwise then that they are well busied, like foode that keepeth life, not else maintaineth strength; yet it hath a pretty mystery in it, that though the gaine scarce prouideth for the Marchants liuelihood, yet the commodities make the land merry : and howsoeuer, I am of the opinion that the former hostile state busied more Sea-men then twice the Trade of *Spaine* can nourish, yet I differ from those that would rather by reprisall make Souldiers, then by nourishing commerce increase Mariners.

Our shipping into *France*, is not such as it hath beene, but nourseth many yong men, or rather sheweth them the Sea, and may busie some seuen or eight hundred men.

Hambrough and *Middlebrough* alwayes haue beene counted the ancient maintainers of Mariners,

ners for the States seruice on all occasions, being ready at hand, and therefore as we wished well to their Shippes, so we desire encouragement to the men. There may be belonging to their employment some foure or fiue hundred Mariners and Sea-men.

Norway and the *Sound* may breed and employ some foure hundred men, those parts being most frequented, those commodities most brought in by the *Hollanders*.

Newcastle voyage is the next, and if not the onely, yet the especiall Nursery, and Schoole of Sea-men: For, as it is the chiefest in employment of Sea-men, so it is the gentlest, and most open to land-men: They neuer grudging in their smallest vessels to entertaine some two fresh-men, or learners; whereas, to the contrary, in the Shippes that voyage to the South-ward, or otherwise, farre out of the Kingdome, there is no Owner, or Maister, that will ordinarily entertaine any land-man, be he neuer so willing, as being bound by their *Charter-partie* to the Marchant, as they say, not to carry but sufficient men, and such as know their labour, and can take their turne at the helme, toppe, and yard. It is by great fauour that others slip in, and they very likely; and therefore whereas in former aduentures I allow them the bringing vp of two or three men in a voyage, it is in generall to be vnderstood, that they were first trained vp, either amongst the Coliers in this iourney: or else came out of Fishermens Boates, and yet but Nouices to those Seas and Saylors, so then this Trade, without all exception, admits of all sorts that neuer see the Sea before: whereby are yearly bred and employed, out of the great store of ships busied therein, some two or three thousand people. A great comfort to youth, and men that want employment, and a great stay to the Sea state, that shall haue need on all occasions of their helpe. I haue shewed my good will enough, being so priuate, to further their employment; and being so ignorant I must not bee bolder.

Island entertainement, asketh and nourisheth some two thousand fiue hundred men; after the number of shipping and barques set downe, and ordinarily employed.

New-found-land may breed and employ some fifteene hundred; but seeing what discouragements they haue, what casualties they are subiect to, we may iudge of their incertainty.

Out of the extraordinary number of all people busied in these two former employments; it is no vnnecessary obseruation, that in any Trade in particular, our coale excepted, our speciall employment, nourishment, and encrease of Sea-men, is euen in this forraine fishing, which I hope will proue but petty, when it commeth to be balanced with our home fishing.

The last Consistance of Shipping propounded, was that of the *East Indies*: which though yongest, was found in shew and state to haue ouer-topped all the rest; as a bird that maketh herselfe gay with the feathers of all other fowles; hauing

hauing borrowed; nay, hauing bought the best Shippes out of other Trades to honour their voyage, and plumed euen *Conſtantinople* her ſelfe, of her ſhipping: therefore that men are entertained extraordinarily in this voyage, it is apparant out of the greatneſſe of the Shipping; the entertainment of them increaſing, it ſhould be a conſequent that Sea-men increaſe this way: But that wee may not by ambages tryumph in their loſſe, or our calamities, wee ſee this way that our Shippes periſh, and therefore our men they ſhrinke. Nay, though ſhippes come home, yet they leaue the men behinde: ſo in this voyage, there is a two-fold way towards our want of Mariners.

In that Shippes, nay great Shippes, are extraordinarily ſubiect to bee caſt away, and then there muſt bee loſſe likewiſe of men; In that though they come, they come home emptied of their men.

By the loſſe of foure Shippes, wee haue loſt at the leaſt foure hundred and fifty men: and in the adventure of ſome three thouſand that haue beene imployed ſince that voyage beganne, wee haue loſt many aboue two thouſand.

Dauid refuſed to drinke of the Well of *Bethleme*, which the ſtrong men had fetched, when he thirſted and longed, becauſe it was the price of blood. This Trade, their commodities are at a far deerer rate, being bought with ſo many mens liues.

But happily ſome will ſay that the greateſt loſſe

E 3   of

of these men was at the beginning, when as all things are difficult: but since our men, framed to a better composition of themselues, to the variety of this Clymate, and heartned to the tediousnesse of this voyage, haue better endured and ouercome those difficulties, and returned more comfortably. Herein the latest voyages will informe vs best, and we will instance it in the three last that haue made returnes.

The first was vnder Sir *Henry Middleton*, whose former gouernment in that kind of voyage, had approued his wisdome and moderation. His ship was that famous and infortunate vessell of eleuen hundred Tun; his company in that ship some two hundred and twenty men. After foure yeares errours vp and downe the sea, wherein he vnderwent many constructions at home, and ouercame strange difficulties abroad; hauing, to his eternall reputation of policy and courage, out-gone the perfidious Turke, and revenged their barbarous wrongs, to the Marchants gaine, and the Kingdomes repute. After He, and his, had, I say, been accompanied with many sorrowes; with labour, hunger, heate, sicknesse, and perill; That worthy Commander, with many a sufficient Mariner, with the whole number (ten excepted) of his liue *Cargazon*, perished in that Acheldama, in that bloudy field of *Bantam*.

Nicholas Dounton, the Vice-admirall of that Fleet returned, and of seuenty he carried forth, brought home some twenty; the rest, their labours and liues were sacrificed to that implacable

The Trades Increase.

East

East Indian *Neptune*: the *Darling* of that voyage is yet there, nor neuer will the Maister, an approued Sea-men, returne, with diuers others.

The second was that of Captaine *Saris*, and Captaine *Towerson*, men formerly exercised in those iourneys, and therefore thought meet to command. Whether they were short of the opinion conceiued of them or no, I know not; if they were, I should attribute part of the losse of their men to their insufficiency, but that the destiny of that country chalengeth it all to it selfe. Captaine *Towerson* who first returned, hauing left behinde him of some hundred and twenty carried forth, fourescore and fiue; and Captaine *Saris*, of some 90 & odde not having brought home aboue two or three and twenty: the *Thomas* of that voyage, which went forth with some 60 men, was brought home by way of a wrecke, you know the destruction of men that name importeth.

The third, that of Captaine *Tho. Best*, Admirall of the Fleete, a man whose former behauiour in Sea-affaires, drew into that iourny with great expectation, and which is very seldome and hard, his carriage in this employment went beyond the great expectation of a reposed demeanour, indulgent to his men, vigilant in his charge, his courage like to his cariage; and his fortune aboue all: he checked the *Indians*, he mated the *Portugals*: those honour our King, these feare his forces: he setled a trade in *Cambaya*, reduced things in order in *Bantam*, brought riches home for the Merchants, and kept reputation for himselfe;

Captaine Pemerton that escaping imprisonment at Moha, iournying in that vnknown Countrey 15 miles by night, got to the sea-side, and finding a small Canow, made a saile of his shirt, and a mast of a stick, and so recouered the ships.

By staying an Armenian ship, wherin at least were some 400 men bound to the Indies, and commaunding the Port, hee drew from thē plain dealing, and made honourable conditions for the Marchants. He encountered foure Gallions, wherein might be some two thousand men.

yet

E 3

yet for all this he had, *Nemesin in dorso*, the Indian vengeance hanted his ship euen to our coasts; of some hundred and eighty men vnder him when he went forth, depriuing him of one hundred and odde men for euer. Some foure or fiue and twenty of the remainder are left, on the desperate account of men, for the Countries facteridge, onely thirty are returned. In two great Sea-fights with the Portugals and their Gallions, which continued foure whole dayes, hee lost not foure men. It was not then the fortune of the warre; neither out of want of ought that victuals and good gouernment could affoord; imputations to some other voyages: Nor had the length of time any fault, part of others bane; he hauing made the voyage in shorter space then any other ordinarily; the dogged Starre of those Clymates, the stench of those Countries were his Fatality.

As one Swallow maketh no Summer, so it is not much to bee maruailed, that in all these voyages some one Ship hath not beene scarred, and not else much hurt in this iourney: She indeed but euen seeing those Coasts, and presently on so great a glut of our men and ships, with the which it seemeth the Sea and Land was then busied and full; when as Captaine *Newport* returned with little losse, and in short time.

Now then as we haue said before, that the Indian shippes die not the ordinary death of Shippes: and that we haue shewen likewise before, that men doe die extraordinarily in this voyage, which is almost incredible: they are distressed likewise after their

their death, and that is very apparant by the meane account made to their heires of what they had in possession in their life time, by what should otherwise be due to them in their purchase, by the calamities of their wiues, children, and friends, after their death. Fabulous and phantasticall Legends haue beene made of the restlesse death of many concealed extortioners, and murderers, whose ghosts haue been said to walke in paine and pennance. On the contrary, how many liue bodies, indeed the true images of the deceased, complain on the death, call for the due of their friends, Fathers, Husbands, Children, Kinsfolkes, and Creditors? Poore *Ratlife, Lime-house, Blacke-wall, Shadwell, Wapping*, and other Sea-townes abroad can sensibly tell. The Marchant he is at home, and therefore he cannot embezell the goods abroad: and it is likely, that what is directly proued due, is paid here to theirs. Then is the calamity of that iourney more fearfull, because out of his owne ill Planet it maketh so many miserable. How this is recompenced it is neither my purpose, nor my part to examine: For certaine there is want of Trade: the *Hollander* would grow greater, if he had all this Trade in his own hands. The Kings customes are now aduanced: This way Shipwrights are set on worke, which must be maintained; and other Mechanical Trades liue hereby, with a number of poore busied. And surely he that would not haue the poore to liue, I would he might begge: And he that would not advance the Kings profite in all liberall manner; and Marchandize is a faire

meanes,

meanes, I would he might dye: and he that regardeth not his Countries good, it is pitty he was euer borne. I desire not, like a second *Phaeton*, to make a combustion. All that I would enforce at this time is, that in this trade our men are consumed, and thereby more want of Mariners. Let the *Straights*-men, and the *Lisbone*-Merchants complaine of their hinderance this way, and say their traffique before was more beneficiall by much, and more certaine to the Custom-house then the Indies be now. Let others report that the foundation of this trade was layd in the ruine of a *Caricke* that Sir *Iames Lancaster* tooke in the first voyage, and that the maine of this after-iollity proceeded of the forced trade driuen with the *Mecha* Fleete by Sir *Henry Middleton*, whereby diuers durst not go presently after to the *Straights*, as the *Angell*, and other shippes, out of rumour of reuenge for violence offered by our *Indian* men to the Turkes in the red sea. Let the common people say that their commodities are vnnecessary: aske the Tradesmen, nay all men, what they haue cheaper: looke into the price of victuals how it riseth out of their great prouisions. Let the whole land murmure at the transport of treasure, and bring in *Charles* the fifth his opinion, speaking to the Portugals of their trade to the East Indies, who said that they were the enemies to Christendome, for they caried away the treasure of *Europe* to enrich the Heathen. Let goe the speech of the small reliefe thereby to the poore, and they whom it doth concerne, may suggest the Indian home state and particular profite

Wherein hee was his owne Trade-caruer out of tenne hundred thousand pounds worth of goods.

Hall Chron. An. 15. Hen. 8.

profite. Once I am sure, that as *Vespasian* the Emperour sayd, He had rather saue one Citizen, then kill one thousand enemies; so his royall Maiesty had rather haue his Subiects, then Custome for them : and you see plainly, that his Maiesties subiects, our country-men, fall this way, and this way is want of Mariners.

Greenland ships, which before I had forgotten, entertaine some Mariners, and helpe to breed others; as of late being fifteene saile, employ some foure hundred men, and may breed of these some fourescore, which helpe somwhat, and may be, by reasonable encouragement, farre more beneficiall, if it be more publique.

And thus we haue runne ouer the materiall trades state and condition in them of sea-men. In all in generall we conceiue want, in regard of the small increase of what is needfull to furnish this great *Machina,* this goodly Engine of our Sea-state, either by supporting their owne members, (the *Newcastle* trade excepted) or all ioyned together, to make vp the great body of our Lands Nauy: witnesse that general presse that was made of men from all the Coasts, to man the shippes that were to attend that matchlesse pearle, that peerlesse Princesse the Lady *Elizabeth* her grace, with her hopefull and happy mate, the illustrious *Palatine,* at their departure ; and our nakednesse that would appeare if there were sudden occasion to furnish some sixe of his Maiesties shippes : all which maketh for the furtherance of our proposition of fishing.

F   The

The third motiue hereto was *Want of Employment.*

As the Cosmographers in their Maps, wherein they haue described the habitable Globe, vse to set downe in the extremity of their Cards, on vnknowne Regions and Climates, That beyond those places they haue noted there is nothing but sands without water, full of wilde beasts, or congealed seas, which no ship can saile, or *Scithyan* liue in: so may I write in the Map of employment, that out of it, without it, is nothing but sordide idlenes, base condition, filling the minde with a hundred Chymeraes and grosse fantasies, and defiling both body and minde with dissolute courses and actions; like fat ground neglected, that bringeth forth a thousand sorts of weeds, or vnprofitable hearbs. And with this disease is our Land affected, our people infected; whereby so many come to an vntimely & reproachfull death in the Land, & many more liue so disolutely, and so wickedly on the seas. I doe not thinke that in any two kingdomes in *Europe*, there are so many Iustized for Murderers and Felons yearely, as in *England*. And aboue all Nations we are most infamous for Pyracies; wherein, against the law of sea-robbers, or at least, besides ordinary example of any other Nation, we forbeare not to prey on our owne Country-men; nay, wee forbeare not our owne acquaintance. Sure the want of grace, and feare of God, is much in most of these: but that men should leaue their wiues, children, and family, and rebel against their owne Soueraignes lawes

lawes, and make warre on all people, proceedeth more out of want of means, want of emploiment at home. Besides, how many that haue more grace, and the same wants, are straightned in their Fortunes, notwithstanding their abilities of body and minde; and are, as it were, damned to pouertie? and more then all these, that haue a litle grace, and lesse meanes, that leade the loathsome life of begging?

Now, if the meanes may be found, nay, if the meanes long found already be offered vnto vs, to redeeme vs out of this disaster, why should wee not vnderstand them? why should we not apprehend them? why should we not be industrious in them? Wee are not those rebellious Israelites that could not see the flowing Land, much lesse enioy it: we haue this place in possession, and if my *Ephemerides* faile me not, I dare say, *Natam inde esse artem*, that shall not onely take away all those discontents and miseries, that want of employment breeds in any of our infortunate countrey-men, but that shall also repaire our Nauie, breed sea men aboundantly, enrich the subiect, aduance the Kings custome, and assure the kingdome; and all this in our owne Seas, by fishing, and especially out of Herring. Towards the which, apparant necessity hauing hitherto made vs the way, we are to perswade you to follow in it by the

Facility,
Profit, and
Vse of this fishng.

The

The Facility, in th at the meanes are in our owne hands.
The Place, our owne seas.
The Art, well knowne.

The meanes in our owne hands, in that we haue all things that shall be vsed about this businesse, growing at home in our owne Land (Pitch and Tarre excepted) whereas the *Hollander*, hauing nothing growing in their owne Land for it, is faine to goe to sixe seuerall Countries, and those remote, and vnder diuers Princes, to furnish themselues, and doe furnish themselues meerely with the barter of Fish and Herring taken out of our seas.

Then the place is not farre remoued, if in our owne Seas, if in his Maiesties Dominions, on the coast of *England, Scotland, Ireland*, is this principall fishing: for by the report of many exercised in this mysterie, and the relation of two especially, painefull herein by their Treatises, *Hitchcockes* and *Gentleman*,

The Herrings first, and towards the ending of Summer, shoote out of the deepes on both sides of *Scotland* and *England*; and beginne to do first so, on the *Scots* coast at Midsummer, when is the first and worst fishing.

The second and best is about Bartholomewtide, from *Scarbrough* in *Yorkeshire*, till you come to the *Thames* mouth.

The third, from the *Thames* mouth through the narrow Seas, but not so certaine, for that extreame weather maketh them shoote on both sides

sides of *Ireland*, likewise on the Coast of *Ireland* is good fishing for Herring, from *Michaelmas* to *Christmas*.

On the North-west seas of *England*, ouer against *Carliel*, about *Wirkentowne*, is good fishing for Herring from *Bartholmewtide* till fourteene daies after *Michaelmas*. So then it appeareth by these reports, that this fishing for Herring is especially on his Maiesties dominions. And to this end aske the ancient custome of the *Hollanders* and *Flemming*, that before they beganne their fishing for Herring, craued leaue of *Scarbrough* aforesayd: which easily obtained, they then layd their Nets. And howsoeuer it pleaseth his Maiesty to allow of his royall Predecessours bounty, in tolerating the neighbour Nations to fish in his streames: yet other Princes take more straight courses. For whereas till *Christmas*, on the coast of *Norway*, called the *Mall Strand*, all strangers do fish, as *Hitchcockes* writeth, they then paid a *youhendale* on euery Last of Herring, to the King of *Denmarke*. And I can likewise remember, that certaine of our Merchants of *Hull* had their goods and Shippes taken away, and themselues imprisoned, for fishing about the Ward-house, and not paying the duty imposed on them by the King of *Denmarke*.

The place, our Seas likewise, for other necessary and profitable fishing: on the Coast of *Lancashire* from Easter to Midsummer, for Cod, for Hakes; twixt *Wales* and *Ireland*, from *Whitsontide* vntill Saint *Iames-tide*, for Cod, and

and Ling about *Padstow*, within the Lands end of Seuerne, from *Christmas* to middle Lent, and in seuen or eight seuerall places more about the Coasts, and within his Maiesties Dominions, the which is largely set downe by *Hitchcockes*.

Now besides this fishing treasure lyeth easily to bee found in our owne Seas, what good Harbours fitting thereto lye open to vs in our owne Coasts, as *Colchester, Harwich, Ipswich, Yarmouth*, with a number of other, set downe painfully by *Gentleman*, together with the commodities they affoord for Timber, Workemanship, furnishing, and harbouring Busses, Nets, and Men?

As the Hauens lye open to vs, as the Seas bee our owne, and as we haue all things almost fitting for such a businesse at home, and naturally, so that nothing may bee wanting to vs but our selues; the Art is well knowne to vs likewise. Maisters for Busses may be had from *Yarmouth* and *Sould*, and the rest of the coasts downe the riuer. Vse maketh Fishermen, and these places affoord store of Seafaring men for the purpose. In *Orford* Hauen and *Alborough* be many good Fishermen, whose abilities exercised in Busses, would (by *Gentlemans* report) put downe the *Hollander*. The like may be sayd of *Sould, Dunwich, Walderswich*, which breede Fishermen. In all these, and many other places, is this rich Art knowne, but not vsed. In all these, and all other, the *Hollanders* swimme like Elephants, we wading like Sheepe. We keep the Bankes and Shoales, when as they are in the depth.

Besides,

Besides, to encourage vs the more, the charges are not great, the paines are not great, the time is not long, the hazard is nothing at all. This is very apparant, and exactly set downe in *Gentleman* his Treatise, whom I shall but obscure to contract; neither is he long.

The next motiue to this fishing, was that of profite; wherein if euer it were true, that a good cause maketh a good Orator, here is a subiect to enable all meane Rhetoricians. Euery man almost is taken with the attention to profite. Loue doth much, but Mony doth all. Here is money, heere is profite in aboundance, and diuers waies. In aboundance, for that the whole charge of a Busse, with all furniture and appurtenances, betweene thirty and forty Last, will cost about fiue hundred pounds: the charges for keeping her a whole summer at Sea, may be some three hundred three score and fiue pounds: the whole Summer filleth her three times, with making one hundred Last of barrels, amounteth to one thousand pounds; wherby, allowing one hundred pounds for weare of ships, and reparations of nets, there is gained fiue hundred sixtie fiue pounds by one Busse in one yeare, and this is after ten pounds the Last, which was so rated in *Hitchcockes* time, which is some thirty three yeres agoe; the *Hollander*, now, selling them for fifteene, twenty pounds, and vpward the Last, at *Danske*. Hence one may gather of the great gaine, that euen riseth to a priuate purse, by this fishing, with a small aduenture, Busses being the maine (and those likely likewise

That is betweene sixtie and eightie tunne.

to

to continue, by Gods grace, some twenty yeares) So then her charges returned for keeping her at sea; the first yeare also she quitteth her own selfe, and there is, I say, fiue hundred sixty fiue pounds, as long as she liueth afterwards, *de claro*. I would faine know, not desiring to be too curious in a strange Common-wealth, but rather to inuite my Countrey-men into this society, what Trade in the Land did euer in his strength promise so much; howsoeuer, neuer any, I am sure, performed so much, so easily, so continually.

When *Antiochus*, in his shew to *Hanniball* of his glorious Army in battel-range, his Elephants being most richly adorned, and all his Souldiers in very braue and costly harnesse and abiliments, willing to draw some acknowledgement from him of his power and strength, asked his opinion of it: the warlike Souldier replied againe, That it was an Armie able to satisfie the most couetous enemy. No question, though the *Carthaginian* noted the people of cowardise; yet it would require great charges, & cost some bloud, to ouercome such an Armie.

In the best Trade in appearance now that is, (and in those Countries certaine there are infinite riches) you see how remote it is, and with what cost of purse, and losse of people followed, yet without such satisfaction. Here is wealth enough to satisfie the most thirsty thereof, without much cost, without any spoyle; euen almost *Salmacida spolia*; if not, *sine sudore, sine sanguine*, and not for a time, but permanent. All other Trades are fetched,

ched as it were, out of a Well, out of the Deepe, I meane from farre, heere is a meere spring which is in superficie hard by vs, out of our owne inexhaustible Sea, from the euer-lasting store of Herring, whence onely the *Hollander* reapeth a million of gold yearely; besides, the most gainefull fishing with other vessels for *Cod* and *Ling*. *Hitchcockes* long agoe discouered the same, his booke is extant; and fore-named *Gentleman* hath very plainly set downe, and in very probable and particular manner disclosed the mysteries thereof. And the conceit the *Hollanders* haue of it, calling it their *Chiefest Trade and Gold-mine*: and the confidence they haue in it, as laying out their Childrens money giuen them by friends, in aduenturing in Busses, and fathers likewise putting in their childrens portions into Busses; presume of the increase that way, and so proportion a summe certaine out of that gaine, in a certaine time; as also that there is for Orphanes laid out, and so increasing that way for the maintenance of them. Here then we may get treasure in aboundance, and certainly; and besides the gaining of it, we shall stay the vnnaturall tide of the departure and transportation of our gold; a mischiefe, which notwithstanding our royall King was sensible of in the raising of it, yet it still departeth with *Vestigia nulla retrorsum*, out of the lazy and disgracious Merchandize of our Coasters, that giue away our coine to the stranger for our owne fish. Which vnseasonable and vnprofitable humor of *Cauponacion*, is this way to be diuerted onely.

G But

But some will say, that our men are not so apt, nor disposed thereto: which cannot be, in regard of the store of Fishermen that our Coasts nourisheth, which liue as hardly, and take as great paines in their fashion; onely wanting the vse of Busses, & seeme to reioyce at the name of Busses, and may on very good reason; for that this Busse-fishing is more easy then any other kind of fishing, which now we vse in Crayers and Punts, as being armed this way better against all weathers, which others suffer and perish in, in other vessels yearly. And as their prouisions are better, and the dangers lesse, so their paines are likewise lesse.

Againe, who will not be exceedingly encouraged with the benefite of such gaine, in so honest a manner, when once the sweete is tasted of, when as otherwise our Countrimen runne such laborious and desperate courses, especially out of want.

Others will say that our Land will not vtter them in any quantity, in regard that the feeding on herring, and fish, doth not taste vs, nor is so receiued as amongst those *Holland* and *Sealand* Mermaids. And sure, if those necessary Lawes prouided by our aduised State, for the keeping of fish daies cleane through our Land were better obserued, it would be more wholesome for our bodies, and make much for the aduancing of our fish, & plenty of other victuals; besides the deerenesse of our fish victuall, which more hurteth our purse then our appetites, for that the price is within this 20. yeares almost trebled, which indeed maketh the

true

true diſtaſt, as all Houſeholders finde, and theron feed their houſholds with fleſh, and otherwiſe; this fiſh victuall being now obtained by Merchandize, which indeed is our owne Staple commodity, whereon groweth this penury to the poore, this great price to others, this diſvſe to all, and in theſe the Kings, the kingdomes loſſe. Yet notwithſtanding there is ſuch quantity of herring, beſides other fiſh, conſumed amongſt vs, that *Hitchcockes* alloweth 10000 Laſts for our prouiſion of herring to be ſpent here in the Realme; ſo that it wold ſaue at home 100000 pounds of treaſure, which to our great ſhame and loſſe, the *Hollanders* carry away, euen for our owne prouiſion: beſides, that prouiſion is of the worſt, ſuch as they call Roopſicke, & ſuch as they are forbidden to bring home. Now to be ſerued of our worſt, whereas we might be our owne caruers, and to giue our gold for that we may haue for nothing; iudge of the loſſe, of the indignity. And as wee may eaſily remedy this by our owne induſtry, ſo we cannot otherwiſe excuſe the fault: our gracious Prince, no queſtion, being ready to aſſiſt vs herein by the ſame fauourable authority which other Trades for their benefite taſte moſt plentifully of, by forbidding the ſale and vttering of herring to his loyall ſubiects by any forrainer or ſtranger whatſoeuer. And in *Holland* it is not lawfull for them to buy any of our Herring, if they be brought thither; Nay, if we bring any thither they are burned. Beſides what other effects of his incomparable clemency would bleſſe our induſtries heerein, hee being

1399 the Art of making cloth, being growne to good perfection, King Henry the 4. firſt prohibited the inuention of forraine-made cloth.

being Lord *Paramount* of these Seas where this fishing food groweth, and which now is taken by strangers? and therefore hee would not questionlesse allow strangers to eate vp the foode that was prouided for the children; the crummes we would not enuy them, though wee are now fed vnder their Table.

Now farther it may be alleaged, that we can vtter no such quantity, nor can affoord no such penyworth. For the first, that must arise out of our diligence. No question we once attaining the Art of the Flemish vsage of these Herring, they will be in as great estimation as the Hollanders, in *Normandy, Nants, Burdeaux, Rochell*, and other such Countries; for which, returne is made of Wine and Woad, for which is alwaies paid ready gold, with a number of other commodities: They will be in as great estimation in the East Countries, *Reuel, Rie, Russie, Danske, Poland, Denmarke*, the returnes whereof are set downe in *Gentleman*. And the quantity of Herring that these fore-named Countries consume is infinite. Therefore though the Hollanders spend more Fish and Herring by much, in their Countries then we do, yet it is their forraigne Trade with all other Nations that is their *Basis*, else they could neuer employ so many Shippes, nor gaine such wealth, or get such strength thereby. And in all these places wee can and doe Trade, and all their returnes wee neede and vse, and therefore may vtter them in as great a quantity as they doe.

Then

Then for the affoording of Herring and Fish at as good a rate as they can, let any consider of the likelyhood in our behalfe. First it standeth with reason, if we haue the like vessels, we can go with as few men: and our fishermen on the Coast, by diuers reports, can liue as hardly as they. And let any iudge of the hardnesse, when the principall time of fishing for Herring is in September and October, and a sixe weekes time, and they are almost in sight of our owne Coasts; and besides good prouision of butter and cheese and Beere, they haue the plenty of the sea-fish: then this way, wee may affoord as good penyworths as they. But I goe further, and say that we haue great vantages of them.

The Seas be our owne, therefore we iourney not so farre as the *Hollander* doth, whereby likewise our trauaile and charge must be lighter: our ports, harbours and roades be at hand; nay, which is more, all *vtensiles* and appurtenances belonging to shipping, as is before shewed (Pitch and Tarre excepted) are found in our owne Land; whereas they with great cost, paines, and hazard, fetch them from sixe seuerall places. So then we shall be able to affoord better cheape then the Hollanders; and so we may sell when they cannot, and so the *English* shall and may weary them, and weare out those flouts wherewith our poore Fisher-men are scorned. For if they bee put by the vttering of their Herrings abroade, they will bee driuen to leaue their great Ships, and fish in smaller vessels neere the shore

You English we will make you glad to weare our old shooes.

shore to serue their owne turnes, as heretofore they haue caused vs to doe; when as likewise on euery tempest they openly triumph ouer vs, for not taking the blessings of God powred into our lappes.

 These hinderances obiected taken away, wee may now resort againe to the sweete fountaine of profite: which besides that it watereth our priuate estates with the continuall spring of great gaine, keepeth in our treasure, which exceedingly now wasteth, bringeth in all commodities that either the East and North Countries, *France*, or *Flaunders*, affoords euen for this barter; it runneth into the sea of the Kings custome: the venting onely of ten thousand Last of Herring beyond sea, commeth to fiue thousand pounds after the rate of the ordinary poundage, besides the custome of Cod and Ling, very neere as valuable as the benefit of Herring, the particular view whereof is set downe by him whom I haue so often named, & in whose booke you may see the greatnesse of the custome amounting to aboue 50000 pound starling, that accrueth to those Countries out of this fishing Trade. And yet all this to them is nothing: their keeping in their treasure, their carrying away our treasure, their aboundance with all other commodities, their greatnesse of their custome this way, is nothing in regard of their profit, honor, safety, that their increase of shipping, increase of Mariners this way begetteth to themselues, amongst all nations, to their state.

 The life of the sea is in shipping, nay one may say

say to ships, *Mare non est mare, vos estis mare.* The beauty of the Sea is in Shipping: and sure the Poets affirming *Venus* to be the daughter of the sea, might meane a Ship by her. For *Hæc vna Venus omnium surripuit Veneri s:* and this little land of the *Hollanders*, exceeded in quantity by *Norfolke* and *Suffolke*, hath gotten this sea, hath gained this *Venus*; *England, Scotland, France,* and *Spaine*, for shipping and sea-faring men, not answerable to them; and all spawned out of fish and fishing.

There hath bene numbred in sight two thousand saile of Busses, and other good vessels, gone out to sea at once of the *Hollanders*: and there hath beene found (by computation) some thirty seuen thousand Fishermen in diuers sorts of vessels at one time employed herein. Hence proceede their great vndertakings, and prodigious aduenturing to all places: hereby they out-goe vs, and ouer-beare all Trades where euer they come. Wee thinke the West-Indie gold to be the cause of the pride and presumption of *Spaniards*: we may assure our selues, that our North Indies counteruaile that treasure, and are the onely confidence of the *Hollander*; euen by breeding sea-men, and increasing of shipping in that aboundance, as that hereby they both swarme euery where, and *France, Spaine*, and the East Countries are full of their shipping. Hence they fetch our coales, and carry them abroad; from *Norway* and *Danske* they bring vs all commodities, and carry forth ours, at a farre better rate then we can our selues: they haue filled *Moscouy*, whence we are emptied, with thither shipping,

shipping; and the *Straights* abound with them, once our possession. They go into, nay they arme in the West Indies where we may not be seene; and in the East Indies they haue had long setled Factories before vs, and haue foure men to one of ours there, and go beyond vs as farre, besides the number in store of goodly shipping; whereby, as they hinder our trade, so they forbeare not (which I cannot but write with stomacke) the honour of our King and kingdome, as presuming somtimes to call themselues *English*, and pretend Embassage, and presents from his Maiesty. Which they did to the King of *Siam*: in other places calling the Crowne and State of *England* into comparison; which made the King of *Achem* aske captaine *Best*, whether the King of *England*, or the King of *Holland*, were the greater Monarke.

Besides, what an infinite number of shippes and men of warre haue they alwayes in a readinesse at home? And as the In-keeper of *Chalets* sayd to his guest, admiring *tantam ferculorum varietatem*, It was with Art all cookt out of pork; this their store, this their aboundance, is raised all out of fishing. Who then would not be moued? who would not be stirred vp therewith? Who would not goe a fishing? You see what want we haue of shipping, what want we haue of Mariners, what discouragements we haue in trades, what wants our men are in. When *Naaman* the *Sirian* complained to *Elizeus* of his leprosie, he was bid wash himselfe in *Iordan* seuen times. He looked for other miraculous courses to be taken by the Prophet, and could hardly

hardly be perswaded thereto, becauſe *Abna* and *Pharphar* (flouds of *Damaſcus*) were better. *Naaman* was a Heathen, and had neuer any experience of Gods *Iordan*: yet hee was in the end perſwaded. To ſupply our wants, to ſatisfie our hunger, to heale our diſeaſes, there is not a riuer, but a Sea, ſhewen vs, and that not in another kingdome, but in our owne; wee are but bidden goe and take fiſh out of it. Wee are Chriſtians, and it is God that hath prouided this remedy: and we ſee by experience no water like ours, and wee ſee our neighbours from every place reſorting thereto, and healing themſelues thereby. You ſee how it concerneth vs; let vs in the end likewiſe be perſwaded. What the number is of our Sea-men, bred and employed by all ſorts of Sea-trades, (our petty fiſhings excepted) may eaſily be gheſt at; and whatſoeuer it may amount to. If out of our whole Land there bee but foure hundred Buſſes built, and ſet forth, of ſeuenty tunne the peece, there are in two yeares nine thouſand Mariners more then was in the Land before: let men of experience and ſtate iudge of the proportion by the way of compariſon, euery one can perceiue the increaſe ſimply. Beſides, by the report of ſome of our beſt Mariners, theſe thus bred, proue not onely equall, but better able then any bred otherwiſe, for Sea-affaires, and publique ſeruice.

On this publik profit of fiſhing thus ſpred abroad the maintenance of Hauens and Hauen townes in *England* beſides, haue no ſmall dependancie, and are ſo materiall to the land, ſo plainly vnderſtood

stood of all his Maiesties subiects; and so well wished to by *Hitchcockes* and *Gentleman*, that it is enough for me but to poynt at them: we all know the vse of them: they shew the decay; and this Art, the reparation and maintenance of them.

The vse of this fishing is implied much in the profite, but more eminent by the consideration againe of the infinite number otherwise of idle people, & out of imployment. Onely by this Art, it is reported not one goeth a begging in all the *Low-countries*; and what a number of people haue we, that, now destitute of meanes, may this way haue a calling? It is a grieuous sin, Idlenesse, and bringeth forth, as we see, horrible effects: to get a liuing by the sweat of our brows, is the ordinance of God, & this way there is a recompence. There were found in *Yarmouth* the last yeare, three or foure hundred, and those of honest disposition, that wanted meanes: & how many hundred more are there in other places, that wold gladly be thus vsed? *Hitchcockes* alloweth to euery one in this imployment, twenty pounds yearely, besides his diet, for his reward, a good sauour to honest men that now haue no meanes; and this onely out of two voyages for Herring. A number of Carpenters and Shipwrights shall be set a work, Coopers busied numbers of people making lines, ropes, cables, dressers of hempe, spinners of thrid, makers of Nets, bred; many salt-houses set vp, besides what store of poore people, all along on the sea-coasts, which are now very poore and idle in *England* and *Wales*, to be vsed in splitting of fish, washing of fish, packing, salting, carrying and re-

carrying

carrying of fish. And on these foresaid occupations depend an infinite number of seruants, boyes & daily labourers, for the vse of things needfull. *Nilus*, whose fertility is enuied, affoordeth not so many sorts of fish, of monsters, as this fishing entertaineth sorts of people: which humbly committing to the high disposer of all hearts, & to the due consideration therby of his Ministers here on earth, I will leaue further to enlarge; and shut vp this abrupt discourse with the allusion of that of *Basil* to this sea-businesse, *Putei dum hauriuntur speciosiores.*

Now for a Corollary to all these imperfect lines: whereas in the superficiall suruey of want of shipping, we find most of our sea-trades, either decaying, or at a stay, let me out of themselues, without offence, propound the consideration of one remedy therto; euen by a *freedom of Traffique* for all his Maiesties subiects to al places. Hereby his maiesties customes will increase, the nauy & sea-men will receiue nourishment out of more imployment, the whole incorporation of marchants reap comfort, in that they may communicate with all aduentures, and the vniversal body of the subiects of the land content, in that they may become merchants; being very ready in this aduentrous world to make new discoueries: whereas now otherwise merchandize, sorting & setled in companies, confineth merchants into those limits that priuate orders tie them in, so that they may not helpe themselues through any discouragements in one trade, but by sute and submission of themselues to the other; though, I say, their trades faile them, and other

ther haue too much: nor may any elſe of the kingdome come amongſt them, though neuer ſo able and well diſpoſed, vnleſſe they come in on ſuch conditions as the victor pleaſeth to propound. A thing in ordinary ſence ſomewhat harſh to fellow-ſubiects, and equall Citizens in this great Monarchie, to be ſo ſeruiceably tyed and ſubiect one vnto the other; and the rather for that thoſe priuiledges, by the indulgencie of the Prince, being granted as a reward to ſome for their induſtries, and exemplary to others incouragements, are ſtrictly vſed to the eternall benefite of a few, and the wrong of all the reſidue.

The *French* company manifeſteth this plainly, which if it had continued (and it beganne but the other day) had vndone all the Weſterne men.

The *Moſcouie* company declareth the ſame, as being granted on condition of ſeruing his Maieſty of all materials (as Flaxe, Oyle, Waxe, Tallow, Cordage) belonging to ſhipping: whereas now it is ſupplyed by ſtrangers, euen ten for one ſhip, and thoſe double our burdens; and notwithſtanding they doe not performe, and haue let fall their Trade, yet none may enter but on their conditions.

The *Greenland* company, out of the pretence of their firſt Whale-hunting, keepe all Fiſhermen, notwithſtanding they knew and vſed thoſe ſeas, from further reſort thither: and ſome Marchants of *Hull* were taken by them in that iourney, and brought backe; notwithſtanding, as I am informed, thoſe countrey-men found it firſt.

The

The *Virginia* company pretend almoſt all that Maine twixt it and *New-found-land* to bee their Fee-ſimple, whereby many honeſt and able mindes, diſpoſed to aduenture, are hindred, and ſtopped from repairing to thoſe places, that either knew or would diſcouer vnfound euen for fiſhing.

The *Eaſt India* men, not able to furniſh thoſe places they reſort to, keepe out other from comming amongſt them, and to looke into thoſe parts they know not, and would giue out of their largeneſſe and riches, entertainment to all the Marchants in the Land. Beſides, how tedious and coſtly they, and all other Companies, make it to their owne Aſſociates, when as out of orders, and cauſe of vpholding their Trade, men can neither diſpoſe of their owne as they would, nor haue the benefite vnder a long time. Beſides, how priuate doe they, and other Companies, make it, when as out of orders and maintaining their Trade, how plentifully ſoeuer the commodities are brought in, and at what advantage ſoeuer they buy them, they will be ſure to keepe vp the price, either by ſending forth moſt part of the commodities abroade, or elſe by buying all others into their hands? that other is hard for the owner ſomtimes, but he doth it in his owne wrong; but to the buyer this is alwaies iniuſt, for that he ſuffereth againſt his will, the common-wealth being made private, ſuffereth by all; this, that, the firſt, and all the more diſcõtentful, in that beſides that all other Nations reſort freely to all thoſe places whence they keepe out their owne Country-men, the like

H 3 faſhion

fashion of Companies and Societies is not vsed in all Christendome else; it being lawfull and vsuall to all other amongst themselues, promiscuously to frequent and communicate with places, and Trades, one by the other. Nay, this separation of Trading, and excepting of Subiects from places, betweene diuers Princes that had but peace one with the other, was so admired and disallowed of, formerly, that *Charles* the 5 Emperour, being moued by the Portugals, being vnder their owne absolute King then, to forbeare the East-Indie Trade, because they had found it; answered, That he had peace with them, and therefore he would haue Trade with them; for they were not his friends, but his enemies, that would hinder him of it. How much more we, murmuring at this iniquity, may affirme that we are all *Britaines*, all subiects to one royall King, all combined together in one naturall league, and therefore not to be barred from trading equally to all places? which his gracious Maiesty, together with the whole assent of the high Court of Parliament, openly professeth, when as there was enacted free liberty for all his Maiesties Subiects, to Trade into the Dominions of *Spaine, Portugall* and *France*, with most sufficient reasons therfore; for the increase of shipping, mariners, thousands of Handicrafts men, of prices of their owne commodities, and augmentation of them, together with the plenty of forraine commodities, & a cheapnesse of them, & the bettering of his Maiesties customes. No one man euer inuented all Sciences, nor any Merchant found all places: yet they make a compensation

Hall.Ann.15. Hen.8.

Ann.3. Iacob.6.

one

one to another. Society first beganne, and knowledge and ciuility, by communication. But if the world in his infancy had beene resolued to haue held priuate what they had in possession, and to haue concealed what they knew, there had not onely been no ciuility, but no society. Yet as the first maintainers of Society had their honour; the first inuentors of Sciences and Arts their rewards; and in all well-disposed States, the Industries of those that do benefit them, haue their encouragements: so is not this my proposition of free Trade otherwise entertained, then that there should be a due respect had of all worthy aduenturers, an especial consideration of the charges and hazard of the first discoueries: which the solertious *Hollander* examples vs, by forbidding their owne Subiects to trade to those places which some particular purse hath, or shall finde out, before that the first Founders haue receiued reasonable benefite of their paines and charges; allowing them some fixe returnes to their owne priuate aduentures, before any else set thitherward. If those aduentures or returnes were increased here for the Finders content, and profit: there is no man would grudge it. But to keepe others out for euer, vnlesse they pay, and submit themselues according to their order, and to their gouernment; or vnder the pretence of one place found to include more then was euer meant; seemes very iniurious. Againe, my Proposition is not any way so tumultuous, as that thereby I would excuse all order and forme of Gouernment in Trades, or otherwise to intend a promiscuous kind of calling, or rather confusion

of

of all sorts. Who knoweth not that the Common-wealth consisteth, *Non ex medico, & medico; sed ex medico, & Agricola?* as also that there must be an Oeconomicall and discreete partition and proportion among the members; Diuers trades, to maintaine the generall body Commerce? I haue onely poynted at some aberrations, but as the Nouice, trauelling through strange Countries, *Tapinando,* or *tanquam canis ad Nilum.* The prosecuting of this Argument would draw on a larger discourse then all the whole former, and would then exceed a Corollary, and detaine the Reader too long. Neither like I the issue of medling, when men tire themselues with controuling of publicke matters, yet many times cannot manage their owne affaires. I make no intrusion into Merchants Mysteries, neither desire to pry into the States secrecie. It was a foolish complaint of the Poet, *Cur aliquid vidi?* it is much more for me to say, *Cur aliquid scripsi?* I am so far from giuing any cause of publique offence, that I would not iustly prouoke any priuate person. I was borne in the Cittie, and liue amongst Sea-men. And as some Almanacke-makers, when they pretend exactnesse in their Calculations, though they doe but roue, vse to appropriate their obseruations to the place they liue in: so I, writing with the same knowledge, would say I desire good to the Meridian of these two places; notwithstanding, as they say also, These may serue alike to all the Land.

FINIS.

THE
DEFENCE OF
TRADE.

In a Letter

To Sir THOMAS SMITH Knight, Gouernour of the EAST-INDIA Companie, &c.

From one of that Societie.

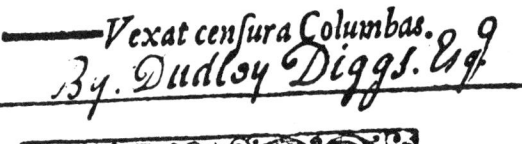

―――*Vexat censura Columbas.*
By. Dudley Diggs. Esq

LONDON,

Printed by *William Stansby* for *Iohn Barnes*, and are to be sold at his shop ouer against Saint *Sepulchres* Church without Newgate.
1615.

TO THE RIGHT
WORSHIPFVLL,
SIR THOMAS SMITH,
KNIGHT, &c.

Right worthy Sir,

When I first heard of an Inuectiue publisht by some vnknowne busie Person, against the *East-Indian Trade*: I must confesse, I held it, *In eorum genere quæ vilescunt spreta*, worthy only of that Companies contempt, whose blest indeuour, with good seruice to the State, hath surely freed them from the poyson. Why should they then regard the hissing of those lurking Serpents, that when the *Itching humour* takes them, will be doing *breuibus & carcere dignum*, euen with the State it selfe?

But hauing since peruscd the *Pamphlet*, I finde vnder the pleasing title of *Increase of Trade*, and gilded ouer with that *Commendable* Proposition of the *Herring*-fishing, a sort of Pills are put to swallowing, that perhaps may worke weake stomacks to distaste our

The Defence

Courfe of *Traffick* by focieties in *London*, efpecially that now of greateft hope and profit to the *Eaſt-Indies*. And though the *Author* handle the particulars with fuch confufed *Contradictions*, as aſſure mee hee conceiued not what he writ: Yet fure, fome *Ape* hath put the *Cats* foot in the fire, fome cunning and malitious perfons, for priuate ends, or *lewder* purpofes infufed the *Quickſiluer* that fet that running head a work. Remembring therefore that a wifeman fhould not onely keep himfelfe from hurt of the *Brute Beaſt*, but feed and clothe, that is as *Plutarch* notes, make profitable vfe of enemies: out of my loue to you that fpend fo much of your *Time*, for the good of the worthie *Marchants* liberall *Aduentures*, to aduance the reputation and reuenue of the *Common-wealth*, I wifh fome one of our Committies beſt experienced in that bufineſſe, would take this oportunitie to fhew how wrongfully they are traduced, whofe voluntarie hazards in fuch long and coſtly voyages, for fuch euen by their enemies confeſſion, dangerous and flow returnes were rather thankefully to be commended.

Good men, well-minded Marchants, while the idle *Drone* and greedie Catterpillers prey vpon the fubſtance of the Subiect here at home, with eating vfurie and harmefull arts, while fuch a Spider in a corner fpends his fruitleſſe dayes perhaps in weauing weake obiections againſt them, from furtheſt parts abroad, they fetch and bring the hony to the Hiue, laborious Bees, they clothe and feede the poore, and giue the willing man imployment to gaine with them, and with the Common wealth, the honour, and the riches that *Venice* firſt enioyed by their *Trade* ouer land

along

of Trade.

along the *Mediterran*, and then the *Portingals* (poore *Portingals* till then) procured by their more aduantagious farre *Sea-trafficke* with those *Easterne* Countries.

This was the first intention, this is still the endeauour of that famous fellowship, best knowne to you that were their first, and are by well deseruing, still their Gouernour; and if it please Almightie God to continue his wondertull blessing, and our good King his gracious countenancing of their industrie, I make no doubt, but by discouery of some neerer passage, or if the worst fall, through the *Aduantage* of our multitude of able bodies, and most commodious *Sea-situation*, euen the way wee haue that rich *Trade* may receiue yet our turne more, and in few yeares a *Staple of Commerce* for all the World be setled in these *Northerne* parts with as much life and quickning to the nauigation and affaires of this whole Iland, as *London* and all sorts of Marchants in it found by one returne from thence last sommer, *Qua nobis placet experientia veri*.

But Sir, this honourable enterprise, like *Hercules* yet in the Cradle, in the infancie hath beene assailed by Serpents slie aspersions, which * *Enuie* long since whispered in the eares of ignorance, of killing Marriners and carrying out the treasure of the land, in answere whereunto had the *East India Marchant* then but told a truth like *Martia's, Bella, Diues, Puella, Fabulla*, hee might haue beene (it may bee iudged) neyther faire nor rich, nor chast, but only forward to commend himselfe: but now when as the poore Snake *Enuie* growes to be a Monster, *Malice*, when the pratler late a creeping Worme is waxt a winged Goose, a setter forth in print of slanders. Now (me thinkes) you are, if

* *Natiua generi humano pestis que vepres nunquam definit in alienis agris licet purgatissimi sint queritare. Pet. Mart.*

The Defence

if not inforft, at leaft inuited happily to fhew the world the well deferuing of that worthie Companie, whofe innocence will fhine more glorioufly euen to the eye obfcur'd of him that dwels fartheft from *London*, by paffing through thofe vapours of an idle or corrupted braine thefe forft or forged imputations.

A worke for truths fake worthie of a feruent fpirits carefull handling: but were it recommended to my weakneffe; though I diflike as much as any man, to fee one, by tranfcribing only in effect, an honeft Gentle- mans good *Fifhing-Proiect, fteale occafion to cenfure all our Trades, and giue intelligence what Shippes of ours, how manned, and at what feafons yearely paffe from place to place, with fuch particulars of our Sea-ftates decay, as muft be eyther true, and fo the fe- crets, or falfe, and fo the flanders of our Countrie.

* *Quæ non vult fic laudari- Nec tali auxilio nec defenforibus iftis--Eget, &c.*

Though I condemne his folly, that proclaimes fuch weakeneffe and fuch want of Marriners and Shipping in our Ports from fond reports of idle fel- lowes, Informations certainly as falfe in thefe particu- lars, as we know they are in our *Eaft-India* matters, ef- pecially at this time, when cleane contrarie, the power and greatneffe of our Royall Mr. and the reputation of his ftrength by Sea and Land, is for the good of Chriftendome, compofing of thofe ftormes which Armies both in *Italy*, and *Germanie* doe threaten.

Though I deteft the hollow-hearted cunning, that doth looke on *Holland*, but yet rowes for other Coun- tries, girding ftill and glancing at our Neighbours of the vnited Prouinces, thofe in reafon of ftate, and through band of Religion, beft affured friends, with

ouer

of Trade.

ouer sedulous insinuating into euery care, their eating vp of our prosperitie, their supplanting of vs in our Trades, and such like seedes of Disaffection, preiudiciall to vs both. Whereas an honest subiect, well disposed in Religion, well affected to the State, would rather rest content with this assurance, that our King hath power enough, when it shall please his wisdome to curbe insolence. Our State may when it will, meet with vnthankfulnesse, and they that made the * Embleme, for their owne good, must be carefull to keepe the Pots from knocking one vpon another.

Their word was, Si collidimur frangimur.

Though more particularly, out of many Touches, I obserue such inclination, such a secret variation in the Compasse of that *Pamphletors* discourse, as makes me very iealous, for all his faire conclusion that hee framed his Almanacke for the Meridian of *Toledo* rather then our Ilands good fortune: witnesse his willingnes to haue vs Trade into those Countries, where wee must bee euer vnder the Lee, in awe and subiect to much inconuenience, rather then make double the profit to our selues and to the Common-wealth by fetching frō the wel-head, from the *Indies*, rather then weaken them, their wealth and shipping, that in all their Moderne Treaties with all Nations shew, how much account they make of that sweet Trafficke.

Though last of all that *Pamphletors* malignant raking vp all sorts of rayling arguments, and spleenefull vrging euery thing against the *East-India Marchant*, might very well prouoke from one of that Societie, the lashes which his often fond excursions fit him for; yet surely I should leaue him to the Riuall-free fruition of those errors, and apply my penne to satisfie an honest

The Defence

nest minde, rather then make him smart or carelesse Readers smile. And as a ground-worke of Integritie, first I would set downe what hee sayes euen in his owne Apparell, Scarfe, and Feather too, As thus.

East Indies. Now followeth the consideration of the East Indie Trade, into whose Seas, not onely the Riuer of Volga, as before you heard, disemboqueth it selfe, but euen the bottome of the Straights is emptied to fill vp those gulfes, and not so onely, but besides that many of our best Marchants haue transported their Staples thither; it hath also begot out of all Callings, Professions, and Trades, many more new Marchants. Then where there is increase of Marchants, there is increase of Trade; where Trade increaseth, there is increase of Shipping; where increase of Shipping, there increase of Mariners likewise: so then rich and large East Indies. The report that went of the pleasing notes of the Swannes in Meander floud, farre surpassing the records of any other Birdes in any other places whatsoeuer, drew thither all sorts of people in great confluence, and with great expectation to heare, and enioy their sweet singing. When they came thither, they found in stead of faire white Swannes, greedie Rauens, and deuouring Crowes; and heard instead of melodious harmonie, vntuneable and loathsome croaking. In indignation that they were so receiued and deceiued, in stead of applauding, they hissed; and of staying, fled away. You are now braue East Indies Meander floud, your Trade is the singing of Swannes, which so many iourney so farre to enioy. God forbid you should bee found so discoloured, and wee so ill satisfied. And howsoeuer that I may bee sure to auoide any detraction, whereby my nature might haue any imputation, or by calling vp more Spirits into the circle then I can put downe againe, I might incurre some danger, and be taxed likewise of indiscretion, for that we onely hitherto haue complained of the want of shipping; we desire now but herein to suruey the store, and see how

you

of Trade. 7

you helpe the increase. You haue built more Shippes in your time, and greater farre then any other Marchants Ships; besides what you haue bought out of other trades, and all those wholly belonging to you; there hath beene entertained by you since you first aduentured, one and twentie Ships, besides the now intended Voyage of one new Ship of seuen hundred Tunne, and happily some two more of increase. The least of all your Shipping is of fourescore Tunne: all the rest are goodly Ships, of such burthen as neuer were formerly vsed in Marchandize; the least and meanest of these last is of some hundred and twentie Tunne, and so goe vpward euen to eleuen hundred Tunne. You haue set forth some thirteene Voyages, in which time you haue built of these, eight new Ships, and almost as good as built the most of the residue, as the Dragon, the Hector, &c. So that at the first appearance you haue added both strength and glorie to the Kingdome by this your accession to the Nauie. But where I pray you are all these Ships? foure of these are cast away, of the which one was of three hundred Tunne, another of foure hundred, the third of three hundred, and the fourth of eleuen hundred; two more are decked vp there as Pinaces to Trade vp and downe: the rest are eyther employed in the Trade in the Indies, or at home out of reparations; which if true, if the Kingdome should haue neede of them on any occasion, it shall surely want their seruice; and so then there is not onely no supply to the Nauie this way, but hurt euen to the whole Kingdome, the Woods being cut downe, and the Ships eyther lost, or not seruiceable. Surely Stories can shew vs, which we may reade in the courses of Common-weales, how tolerable, nay how laudable it is in all States, to enlarge Commerce. Marchants, whome wee should respect, can tell vs of the casualties which not onely the Shippes but their Estates are subiect to by auentures. Mariners, whom we must pittie can teach vs of the ordinary dangers not onely that Shippes and goods, but their liues are subiect to by Sea. I must not then exprobrate

brate that to them which is to be imputed to the Sea; nor are they to bee blamed out of reason for that which deserueth in humanitie, commiseration; nor is England bounded by our Horizon, to goe no further then wee see. Wee haue learned long since, that Mercatura si tenuis sordida, si magna, splendida: the Stranger the Countrie, the greater the aduenture; the more famous our Nation, the more worthie the Marchant. Before wee were, euen Horace writ, Currit Mercator ad Indos. Loath then am I to borrow that saying of Demosthenes on his courting of Lais, to pay it to the Indian Trade, by alleaging, that Non tanti Emam pœnitentiam, only hauing now in common that Roman Prouiso, Ne quid detrimenti Respub. capiat. Let vs examine that which may moove patience, that our Woods are cut downe, and the Ships either lost or not seruiceable: Our Woods, I saie, cut downe in extraordinarie manner, neither doe the Ships die the ordinarie death of Shippes. Our Woods extraordinarily cut downe, in regard of the greatnesse of the Shipping, which doth as it were deuoure our Timber. I am able out of sufficient testimonie to affirme, that since the Indian Trade, and mœrely through their building of their Ships of so great burthen, and their repairing, (the building notwithstanding beganne but fiue yeares since) that Timber is raised in the Land fiue shillings, and more, in the load, nay, almost not to bee had for monie, which the Companie (no question) being sensible of, very wisely séeke to helpe themselues in, by building of Ships in Ireland for their seruice: yet it seemeth their incouragement that way, is but necessitous, in regard by their owne saying, besides the hazard, the charges are little lesse; and which is worse, that kind of Timber is but vntoward for that vse, being so extreame heauie, that a Ship of a small burden draweth much Water. In fiue yeares space their building, together with their repairing of Ships almost equall to building, beget such a scarcitie, what will a little continuance bring forth? Bring forth I cannot say ought, but a priuation will follow euen of all our

of Trade.   6

our Timber Wood. The Kings Nauie must be maintained, other Merchants of lower ranke must haue shipping, and the Sea-trade may increase, and then eyther we must Trade without shipping, or make Shippes without Timber.

When the Norman Conqueror hauing subdued the most part of the Kingdome, passed from Essex into Kent, which then made head against him, the Kents, hauing by the aduice of their politike Bishoppe and their stout Abbot, cut downe great boughes, and with them in their armes marched towards the Conqueror; whereby, besides the nouzltie of the sight, the Armie appeared double as bigge: William himselfe so conceiuing it, as also amazed to see Woods walke; more feared and discontented with that sight, then otherwise assured with his former successe, condescended to what demands soeuer were made by those people, to haue such weapons laid downe, and to gaine such ingenious Subiects; whereby, to their eternall benefit, and credit, their persons were neuer in bondage, nor their Lawes altered. In this their Land-Stratageme, I see our Sea-Arts, in that and these Woods being the fatall instrument of our fortunes, Boughes of Trees kept the Kentish-men out of seruitude, when they held them in their hands, and but for shew; their bodies will keepe vs in libertie when they containe vs, and are for seruice, and by their moouing on the water they will amaze both French and Spanish, and whomsoeuer, and keep them, and all others, from comming neere vs: Out of which prouident fore-sight, our most worthy Princes formerly raigning, haue made diuers Lawes in fauour of Timber Trees: and our most noble King hath prouided thereto with new arressiors for the preseruing and increasing of them; but that a parricide of Woods should thus be committed by building of Shippes, it was neuer thought on by any of our Royall Solons, and therefore there was no prouiso for it: Nay, this inconuenience was so little suspected, that our said famous Princes haue prouided cleane contrarie, with great bountie and indulgence,

*35. Hen. 8. 17. 13
Elizabeth. 25.*

Forbidding by proclamation the building with Timber

C

gence haue encouraged by reward out of their owne purses the builders of great Ships; as bestowing on the builders fiue shillings on the Tunne for euery Tunne that is builded aboue one hundred Tunne in a Ship; so necessary did the Prince thinke his maintenance of shipping, the accession thereof consisting much in their greatnesse, to the honour and safetie of the Kingdome; and such vse he made account he should haue of them. Whereas now this waie he contributeth, to the spoile of his Woods, to the losse of the Shippes, and to the hurt of the Kingdome. I heard a Shippe-wright say on the losse of the Trades Increase, that if you ride fortie miles from about London, you could not find sufficient Timber to build such another. It was a Ship of eleuen hundred Tunne: for beautie, burthen, strength, and sufficiencie, surpassing all Marchants Ships whatsoeuer. But alas! shee was but shewne, out of a cruell destinie shee was ouertaken with an vntimely death in her youth and strength, being deuoured by those Iron Wormes of that Countrie, that pierced her heart, and brake many a mans withal memorable in her misfortune, onely redounding to the Common-wealthes losse. For as for the Marchants, though I pittie their aduentures with all my heart, yet in this their part of losse was least; for all their goods were on shore; and shee had brought aboundance out of the Mecha Fleete, which shee did both tithe and toll : And thanks be to God, they are more then serues by what is returned from her, and more then that often, by the grace of God, will come from her to the Marchants gaine.

The like vntimely fall had the other three of great burthen, gallant Ships, neuer hauing had the fortune to see their natiue soile againe, or the honour to doe their Countrie any seruice, in respect of all other ships that wander ordinarily to other Countries, therefore I may iustly say that they die not the ordinary death of shippes, who commonly haue some rest, and after long seruice die full of yeares, and at home, much of their timber seruing againe

to

of Trade. 11

to the same vse, besides their Iron-worke, and the rest o-
therwise seruiceable, and not in this bloudie and vnseasonable fashion, rather indéed as coffins full of liue bodies,
then otherwise as comfortable ships. For the rest that liue, *Our Ships are*
they come home so crazed and broken, so maimed and vn- *fain to take in*
manned, that whereas they went out strong, they re- *the natiues of*
turne most feeble: and whereas they were carried forth *the Indian*
with Christians, they are brought home with Heathen. *Countries to*
What the profits are to the Marchants, for so great an ad- *supply the*
uenture, I know not. I am sure amends can not easily be *wants of our*
made for so great losse, euen in this point which is our spe- *dead Sea-men*
ciall subiect, for wast of Woods, and spoile of shipping. *to bring home their Ship.*

The last cōsistance of shipping propounded, was that of
the East Indies: which though yongest, was found in shew
and state to haue ouer-topped all the rest; as a Bird that
maketh her selfe gay with the feathers of all other Foules;
hauing borrowed, nay, hauing bought the best ships out of
other Trades to honour their Voyage, and plumed euen
Constantinople her selfe, of her shipping: therefore that
men are entertained extraordinarily in this Voyage, it is
apparant out of the greatnesse of the shipping; the entertainment of them increasing, it should be a consequent that
Sea-men increase this way: But that we may not by ambages triumph in their losse, or our calamities, we sée this
way that our shippes perish, and therefore our men they
shrinke. Nay, though ships come home, yet they leaue the
men behind: so in this Voyage, there is a two-fold way
towards our want of Mariners.

In that Ships, nay great ships, are extraordinarily subiect to be cast away, and then there must be lost likewise of
men; In that though they come home emptied of their
men.

By the losse of foure ships, we haue lost at the least foure
hundred and fiftie men: and in the aduenture of some thrée
thousand that haue beene imployed since that Voyage beganne, wée haue lost many aboue two thousand.

David refused to drinke of the Well of Bethelem,
C 2 which

which the strong men had fetched, when hes thirsted and longed, because it was the price of bloud. This Trade, their commodities are at a farre dearer rate, being bought with so many mens liues.

But happily some will say, that the greatest losse of these men was at the beginning, when as all thinges are difficult: but since our men framed to a better composition of themselues, to the varietie of this Climate, and heartned to the tediousnesse of this Voyage, haue better endured and ouercome those difficulties, and returned more comfortably. Heerein the latest Voyages will informe vs best, and wee will instance in the their last that haue made returnes.

The Trades Increase. The first was vnder Sir Henrie Middleton, whose former gouernment in that kind of Voyage, I so approoued his wisdome and moderation. His ship was that famous and infortunate Vessell of eleuen hundred Tun; his company in that ship some two hundred and twentie men. After foure yeares errors vp and downe the Sea, wherein he vnder-went many constructions at home, and ouercame strange difficulties abroad; hauing, to his eternall reputation of policie and courage, out gone the perfidious Turke, and reuenged their barbarous wrongs, to the Marchants gaine, and the Kingdomes repute: After Hee, and his, had, I say, beene accompanied with many sorrowes, with labor, hunger, heate, sicknesse, and perill; That worthie Commander, with many a sufficient Mariner, with the whole number (ten excepted) of his line Cargazon, perished in that Acheldama, in that bloudy field of Bantam.

Captaine Pemerton that escaping imprisonment at Moha, journeying in that vnknown Countrie 15. miles by night, got to the Sea-side and finding a small Canow, made a saile of his shirt, and a mast of a stick, and so recouered the Ships.

Nicholas Dounton, the Vice-admirall of that Fleete returned, and of seuentie he carried forth, brought home some twentie; the rest, their labors and liues were sacrificed to that implacable East Indian Neptune: the Darling of that Voyage is yet there, nor neuer will the master, and approued sea-man, returne, with diuers others.

The second was that of Captaine Saris, and Captaine Towerson, men formerly exercised in those iournies, and there—

of Trade.

therefore thought meet to command. Whether they were short of the opinion conceiued of them or no, I know not; if they were, I should attribute part of the losse of their men to their insufficiencie, but that the destinie of that Countrie challengeth all to it selfe. Captaine Towerson, who first returned, hauing left behind him of some hundred and twentie carried forth, some score and fiue; and Captaine Saris of 90. & odde not hauing brought home aboue two or three and twentie: the Thomas of that voyage, which went forth with some 60. men, was brought home by way of a wreck, you know the destruction of men that name importeth.

The third, that of Captaine Thomas Best, Admirall of the Fleet, a man, whose former behauiour in sea-affaires drew into that iourny with great expectation, and which is very seldome and hard, his carriage in this employment went beyond that great expectation of a respect deuotion, and indulgent to his men, vigilant in his charge, his courage like to his carriage, and his fortune aboue all, hee checked the Indians, he mated the Portugals: those honor our King, those feare his forces, he setled a trade in Cambaya, reduced things in order in Bantam, brought riches home for the Marchants, and kept reputation for himselfe; yet for all this, he had Nemesin in dorse, the Indian vengeance haunted his ship euen to our Coasts; of some hundred and eightie men vnder him when he went forth, depriuing him of such vndred and odde men for euer. Some foure or fiue and twentie of the remainder are left, on the desperate account of men, for the Countries Facteridge, onely thirtie are returned. In two great Sea-fights with the Portugals and their Gallions, which continued foure whole dayes, he lost not foure men. It was not then the fortune of war; neyther out of want of ought that victuals and good gouernment could affoord; imputations to some other Voyages: Nor had the length of time any fault, part of others bane; he hauing made the voyage in shorter space then any other ordinarily; the dogged Starre of those Climates, the stench of those Countries were his fatalitie.

By staying an Armenian ship, wherin at least were some 400 men bound to the Indies, and commanding the Port, hee drew from thē plaine dealing and made honorable conditions for the Marchants. He encountered foure gallions, wherein might be some two thousand men.

C 3

As one swallow maketh no summer, so it is not much to be marvailed, that in al these Voyages some one ship hath but béene scarred, and not else much hurt in this iournie: Shée indéed but even séeing those Coasts, and presently on so great a glut of our men and ships, with the which it séemeth the sea and Land was then busied and full: when as Captaine Newport returned with little losse and in short time.

Now then as wée haue said before, that the Indian ships die not the ordinary death of ships: and that wée haue shewen likewise before, that men doe die extraordinarily in this Voyage, which is almost incredible: they are distressed likewise after their death, and that is very apparant by the meane account made to their heires of what they had in possession in their life time, by what should otherwise be due to them in their purchase, by the calamities of their wiues, children, and friends, after their death. Fabulous and phantasticall Legends haue béene made of the restlesse death of many concealed Extortioners, and Murderers, whose Ghosts haue béene said to walke in paine and penance. On the contrary, how many liue bodies, indéed the true Images of the deceased, complaine on the death, call for the due of their friends: Fathers, Husbands, Children, Kinsfolks, & Creditors: Poore Ratlife, Limehouse Blacke-wall, Shadwell, Wapping, and other sea-townes abroad can sensibly tell. The Marchant hée is at home, and therefore hée cannot embezell the goods abroad: and it is likely that what is directly proued due is paid here to theirs. Then is the calamitie of that iournie more fearefull, because out of his owne ill Planet it maketh so many miserable. How this is recompenced it is neyther my purpose, nor my part to examine: For certaine there is want of Trade: the Hollander would grow greater, if hée had all this Trade in his owne hands. The Kings Customes are now aduanced: this way Shipwrights are set on worke, which must be maintained; and other Mechanicall Trades liue hereby, with a number of poore busied.

And

of Trade.

And surely hee that would not haue the poore to liue, I would hee might begge: And hee that would not aduance the Kings profit in all liberall manner; and Marchandize is a faire meanes, I would hee might die: and hee that regardeth not his Countries good, it is pittie hee was euer borne. I desire not, like a second Phaeton, to make a combustion. All that I would enforce at this time is, that in this trade our men are consumed, and thereby more want of Mariners. Let the Straights-men, and the Lisborne-Marchants complain of their hinderance this way, and say their Trafficke before was more beneficiall by much, and more certaine to the Custome-house then the Indies bee now. Let others report that the foundation of this Trade was laid in the ruine of a Carick that Sir Iames Lancaster tooke in the first Uoyage, and that the maine of this after-iollitie proceeded of the forced Trade driuen with the Mecha Flæt by Sir Henry Middleton, whereby diuers durst not goe presently after to the Straights, as the Angell, and other ships, out of rumor of reuenge for violence offered by our Indian men to the Turkes in the Red sea. Let the common people say that their commodities are vnnecessarie: aske the Tradesmen, nay all men, what they haue cheaper: looke into the price of victuals how it riseth out of their great prouisions. Let the whole Land murmure at the transport of treasure, and bring in Charles the fifth his opinion, speaking to the Portugals of their Trade to the East Indies, who said that they were the enemies to Christendome, for they carried away the treasure of Europe to enrich the Heathen. Let goe the spæch of the small reliefe thereby to the poore, and they whom it doth concerne may suggest the Indian home state and particular profit. Once I am sure, that as Vespasian the Emperor sayd, Hee had rather saue one Cittizen, then kill one thousand Enemies; so his Royall Maiestie had rather haue his subiects, then Custome for them: and you sœ plainly, that his Maiesties subiects, our Countrie-men, fall this way, and this way is want of Mariners.

Wherein hee was his owne Trade-caruer out of tenne hundred thousand pounds worth of goods.

Hall chron. An. 15 Hen. 8.

Now

The Defence

Now Sir, imagine that you were the Reader to bee satisfied, and you shall see, how while the froth of his *Meander* floud and such like following fuming stuffe euaporates it selfe, out of the residence, Drosse as it is, I will extract all his Obiections, which now like folded sheepe, or as raw Souldiers in a rout, stand faces euerie way, but I will put them in aray, in order Sir, and yet defeat them, fairely as I goe.

First, comes a very forlorne Hope, two light, slight charges, were they true, of the Riuer *Volga* disimboquing, and the *Straights* emptying, but I wil take the former rather from the fifth page of his Booke where he speakes English.

The first Obiection. The marchant formerly trading Russia, hath for warmth and profit seated himselfe in the East Indies, and transported thither much of the Muscouie Staple, &c. To which I answere.

Answere. IF here, as some imagine, hee haue look't asquint vpon Sir *Thomas Smith*, an Honourable Gentleman, whose constant and continuall readinesse to spend both time and monie in any action that may good the Common-wealth, doth merit as much praise as modestie may giue a liuing man: How much is hee to blame, to wrong a worthie member of this Citie of the Kingdome, that (besides many other publike businesses) hath beene long, and is still Gouernour of the *Muscouia* Companie, and with them continually as great a Venturer as any? If he intend it by the Companie, how ignorantly doth hee taxe that bodie, the * Discouerers of the *Northerne* World, that all the last

* With the expence of 120000. pouds in discoueries onely.

of Trade.

last age honoured our whole Nation with their famous Nauigation, that farre from letting fall their Trade, after so many yeares of losse by reason of the troubles of that Land, doe yet make good a stocke, not onely to [a] defend [b] their fishing of the Whale in *Greeneland*, against all other Nations, but at this present able to beare the charge of sixe or seuen thousand pounds extraordinarie, to defray a *Muscouite* Ambassador al the last Winter here, and Sir *Iohn Merrick*, one of ours now there, in hope to settle once more Priuileges for our Nation, and in time to bring ouer the *Caspian Sea* along that Riuer *Volga*, whose name (it seemes) he onely knowes, a Trade for *Indico* and *Silke* so rich, that the *East India* Marchant may perhaps bee glad for so much to ioyne purse with them.

[a] With twice as many ships, as they need send for fishing.
[b] At their charge it was first discouered, and by their great charge *Viscaniers* sent for, and our Natiō taught to kill the Whales.

His second Obiection is of the Streights emptying, &c. or from his sixth Page. **The Trade into the bottome of the Streights is lessened by the Circumuention of the East Indie Nauigation, which fetcheth the Spices from the Well-head, &c.** but marke,

The second Obiection.

IF this he sayes were true, so long as by the change the Kingdome gaine, and onely *Turkes* doe lose, of what faith is hee that complaines? The *Turkie* Marchant is too honest and too wise, he knowes that when the great *Imbargo* and the warre that followed with *Spaine*, had forc't vs from the Marchant-strangers hand, to take our Spices (which were fetched from *Lisbone* formerly) [e] at extreme rates, His wittie Predecessor plotted, by his Factors, with the *Carauan*, to bring those Spices to *Aleppo* ouer Land, and so a-while did helpe to serue the subiect here at lower prices,

The Answere.

[c] As when lowest Pepper eight shillings a pound, &c.

D

ces, vntill the *Hollander*, by the *Cape Buena Esperanza* found the meanes to bring such store of those Commodities, that the [d] low price beat the *Streights* Marchant from that [e] Marchandize: And then our Marchants, (that what euer ill men say, do scorne to weare the shooes of other Nations) resolu'd vpon an *India Voyage* for themselues, with foure good Ships, & some of them that wanted now imployment to the *Streights*: by the returne whereof, and by continuance of that Trafficke, our Spices are not onely cheaper to vs * halfe in halfe, but the *Straights* Marchant, long before this Pamphlet was put forth, out of our ouerplus hath serued the *Turkes* with Spice, and [f] carried in one yeare much more into the *Streights* then euer was imported thence: The proceed whereof, as *Turkie* Marchants know, besides the increase of shipping to export it, will returne Wares, to imploy at least twice as much shipping more: so much hath God Almightie blest vs, if we can bee thankefull. So opposite to truth is all he sayes of the *East India Trades* decaying of the *Streights*.

Besides, if the *East India* Marchant (that would he looke at priuate profit onely, can imploy his stock for swifter, and for surer, and perhaps more gaine) should, through discouragement of such malignant tongues, now giue that Trafficke ouer, liues there any (in the Citie among Sea-men) else so simple, as to thinke, that while the *Dutchmen* hold their Trade, there will bee any more Spice brought from *Turky*? Certainely that course is now for euer ouerthrowne, and so I thinke, are these two forlorne accusations.

Next then, to ouerpasse his Fireworkes of triumph onely

---

[d] Though not vnder foure shillings the pound for Pepper, &c.
[e] Which when it was at best, imploied not passe 200. Tun of shipping yearely.
* As Pepper 2. shillings the pound when dearest, &c.
[f] Of that which came home 1613. alreadie 2628. bagges of Pepper, 5549. of cloues 21-0. of Nutmegs, &c. which imploi'd outward at least 600. Tun of shipping & will fraight at least twice as much home.

only, before Victorie, after some crackling noise, and no hurt, his Vantgard comes vp vpon our *East-India* Nauie, and like one of the wise Captaines of old time, he would cosen his Souldiers with false enumeration of their strength; I will therefore disproue him with a truer Catalogue of their ships.

Per Tonne & Tonnage.

The *Dragon* —— 1060. { An old worne ship bought by the Companie, but by their cost made so strong, that shee is now gone her fifth voyage to the *Indies*.

The *Hector* —— 800 { An old ship bought too, and made new and warlike, and now gone her 5. voiage too.

The *Suzan* —— 400. { A very rotten ship, when shee was bought, and likely to haue beene broke vp for firewood, yet she made one voyage, and in her second, foundred in the Sea, as wee thinke.

The *Ascension.* —— 400. { An old ship bought, Ordinance, Tackle, Furniture, and all for fiue hundred pound, shee yet made two voyages, and in her third was wilfully runne aground vpon the sholes of *Cambaya*

D 2 The

Per Tonne & Tonnage.

The Consent — 150. { A bought ship, she brought home Cloues, &c. but being found too litle, was sold away.

The Vnion — 400. { An old Hulke, bought from carrying Masts and Dele, yet made a warlike ship, and lost in *Brittanie*.

The Expedition — 320. { Gone out her third voyage.

The Trades Increase 1293 { New built, and ouerswaid as she was careening at *Bantam*, &c.

The Peppercorne — 342. { New built, and now gone her second voyage.

The Darling — 150. { New built, and now Trading and discouering in the *Indies*.

The Globe — 527. { Bought and Rebuilt for Trade and Discouerie in *Bengala*, whence shee is not yet returned.

of Trade.

Per Tonne & Tonnage.

The Cloue ———— 527. { She was at *Iapan* with Captaine *Saris*, a new strong ship, and going againe her second Voyage.

The Thomas ——— 342. { New built and gone her second Voyage.

The Iames ———— 600. { New built, but not yet returned from the *Indies*.

The Oceander ——— 213. { New built, and not yet returned.

The Salomon ——— 400. { And now gone her second Voyage.

The Concord ——— 213.) (Gone out lately.

The new yeares gift — 867.) (New built of *Irish* Timber.

The Hope ———— 533.) (New built in *Ireland*.

The Samaritan ——— 543.) (

The Thamazin ——— 133.) (New built.

The Aduise ———— 160.) (New built.

The Lyon ————— 386.) (

The Great Defence-400 {Readie to goe out with the Cloue.

And two more now building at *Depford*, one of 1100. Tunne, the other of 900. Tunne, &c.

Out of these ships, the Companie haue set forth alreadie 17. voyages. Neither may he excuse his mentioning only 13. with pretence of his bookes being written long before his friend (no doubt) put it forth, since in the booke hee speakes of Captaine *Saris* returne, &c. But let that passe. What saies he to these ships?

Pag. 29.

The third objection.
Foure of these ships are lost, and that not by the ordinarie death of ships. The Trades Increase, that gallant shippe, was ouertaken by vntimely death in her youth and strength, being denoured by those iron-hearted wormes of that Countrey, &c. The like vntimely fall had the other thrægallant ships, neuer hauing had the fortune to see their natiue soile, nor the honour to doe their countrey any seruice, &c.

Answere.
And is foure of so many ships, so long at Sea, so great a losse, especially in fourteene yeares of our yet infant and discouering trade, while in the farthest and vnknowne parts of the world

— *Ignari hominumq́ locorumq́,*
Erramus, vento vastis & fluctibus acti,
Incerti quo fata ferant, vbi sistere detur, while we seeke for trafficke with strange Nations? Surely wee esteeme it Gods great blessing, that wee lost no more, and wee are thankfull for it. He hath not dealt

so

so with some other Nations. Looke on the *_Portin-_ *What worke would hee make, if wee should lose so much wealth, and so many men, in so lamentable a manner as the _S. Iohn_ or _S. Benoit_, Carrickes of _Portingal_ were cast away
gall or _Dutch_ beginnings. Nay now they are so well experienc't, the first lost in a manner all their _China_ Fleet and riches very lately, in returne to _Goa_; and the other, the very last yeare, out of foure ships richly laden, the returne of many more set forth, saw the ruine, ships, goods, men and all, of two; and one of them euen at their doores in ᵐ _Holland_. And if this Vulture that thus followes wreckes and dead mens bodies, should but reckon other Marchants losses in m At the _Testsil._
that time, which I had rather pitie, he would, it may be, in his so approued _New-castle_ coasting course, finde as great losse of Mariners and shipping.

And for the extraordinarie death, I know not well what he intends: but sure the Companie, euen in the losse of most of them, for some things, found Gods extraordinarie blessing. Witnesse a true narration.

First, for the _Trades Increase_, when that thrice-worthie Generall Sir _Henry Middleton_ (that neither tithed nor tolled the _Mecha_ Fleet, as malice would haue men beleeue, but like true Iustice, with the Sword and Ballance in his hand, made the beginning, laid the true foundation of our long desired _Cambaya-Trade_) had made the false _Turks_ pay for his most barbarous imprisonment at _Moha_, he conceiued, a twelue moneths stay, by that misfortune, longer forth, might peraduenture bring his shippe in danger, and therefore more for prouidence then need, hee purposed to careen her at _Bantam_, our then greatest Factorie, where he was no stranger. But such was Gods good pleasure, as it hath done here, and may doe any where, a mortal and infectious sicknesse raged there among the natiues

tiues of that land, and fell on him and many of his people vnto death, so as the shippe (that by the breaking of a Cable ouer-swaied) was left halfe ruind aboue water, for want of skilfull hands to helpe her.

Yet the goods were safe.

The *Ascension*, though an old Shippe bought, made for the Companie two voiages to *India*; but in her third, by the wilfulnesse of a lewd Master, that would not suffer a Pilot to be entertained, shee was runne aground vpon the sholes of *Cambaya*, where yet all the men, with the best marchandize, were saued.

The *Vnion*, bought from carrying Masts and Dele, was by their cost made warlike, and so strong, that notwithstanding her vnhappie losse of the Captaine, and eleuen more of her principall men, through foolish breach of their * commission, yet shee had come richly laden home, if first a mutinie had not fallen among those new vnfit Commanders, and then fourteene of her ablest men had not forsaken her distrest, to goe for *Rochell* with a shippe of *Alborough*. And yet, good shippe, almost at home vpon the Coast of *Brittanie*, where shee droue in with her weake men, the lewd Inhabitants first drew her on the Rockes, then boared her full of holes, and with more difficultie farre then would haue saued her, made a wrecke, as since vpon their execution for it, some of the actors haue confest in *France*.

In going on land at Gongomora in the Island of S. Laurence, contrarie to expresse instructions.

The fourth and last, was the old rotten shippe, the *Susan*, ready to haue beene broken vp for fire-wood, when the *East-India* Marchant bought her for their voyage, which shee yet performed, though in returning home vpon her second voyage, shee foundred in the

the Sea, as men suppose: so that (as *Neptune* in the Poet said)

Vnus erit amissum tantum quem in gurgite quærent, Vnum pro multis, &c.

This only one shippe properly was lost. Now let him then but reade what hee hath written of these ships, and if he can forbeare to blush.

I but the rest of their ships are either out in the Voyage, or here at home out of reparations, returning so crazed and broken, &c. that if the Kingdome should haue need on any occasion, it shall surely want their seruice, &c. And this in truth is an obiection worthie of an answere.

The fourth obicction

Although before this Trade grew quicke, the Companie had leisure, and were forced to new-build, and bestow great cost vpon their old bought ships; yet now for diuers yeares, since they built new, there is no shadow of a truth in that hee saies: for that their ships, some after two yeares and a halfe, some after three, and longer voyages, come home so strong and seruiceable, that without cost of Planke or Timber (except only sheathing, due to euery Marchants good shippe, and performed easily in thirtie daies) they haue beene found fit to send out againe vnto the *Indies*. And thus without new building

Answered.

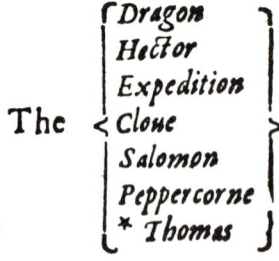

The
{ Dragon
Hector
Expedition
Clove
Salomon
Peppercorne
*Thomas }
was only dock't and sheath'd for the new Voyage.

*This ship hee saies came home by way of a wreck, is it not likely?

And that this point of sheathing may bee fully vnderstood, The *Cloue* one of the greatest, that had been at *Iapan* longest and farthest out, was for a triall sheathed and fitted perfectly in fourteene dayes: who then can doubt of their abilitie to serue the State at home vpon our Coasts, or at the most, little aboue a Summers Voyage out?

The fifth Obiect.

But they are not bare, &c.

Answere.
*How much is the whole Kingdome bound vnto him for his care, not onely with infinite charge to keep his royal nauy in better state then euer, but to worke out wisely such addition of strength in shipping euen from his Marchants?

YEs commonly six Moneths, and when our Nauie is compleat, and our Trade setled, by Gods grace we shall haue many ships returning euery Summer, as well as those preparing in the Winter to goe forth: and see this mans ill luck, euen this last mustering yeare, before the putting out of that same Pamphlet, besides those seuen aboue set-ships. The *Samaritan*, the *Lion*, and the great *Defence* lay many moneths within the Riuer, readie, if neede had beene, to doe the seruice which his Maiestie in his Princely wisedome * prouides for, in his letters Patents of the Companies Incorporation.

Tenne goodly shippes and such as (not to meddle with our Marchants ships, our friends at home) being
all

all together, well prouided of munition and men, would not much feare the Royall Nauie of some Kings in Christendome. A Squadron that within our narrow Seas, hauing the Land and Ports to friend, might stop the furie of another selfe cónceited inuincible *Armado* : what meanes this poore man then to write hee knowes not, and it seemes, hee cares not what?

I thinke our *Kentish* boughes that got vs Gauel-kind of the *Conqueror*, like Bees in his brains haue made him wood : In a wood I am sure he is now, & like to lose himselfe, for his next forces, like *Benzo* his naked *Indians* come to fight *Ligneis Telis*, with woodden Arguments. But any Wood will serue his rancor for Arrowes to shoot at the *East India* Companie: and would hee flie into the *Irish* bogges, as hee doth into their Woods, I must now pursue him. Hee sayes,

> Our Woods are extraordinarily cut downe, in regard of the greatnesse of their shipping, which doth, as it were, deuoure our Timber, &c. King Henry the eight, and Queene Elizabeth, by Lawes, and our King by Proclamation, sought to preserue and increase our Woods, but that a parricide of Woods should thus bee committed, by building of Ships, &c. and so on, but

The sixth Obiection.

Thinkes he, these royall Princes cared to keep their Woods for any nobler vse, then to build gallant ships, and those not to lie still and rot his ordinarie death, but such as round about the World disperse the honour of the Crowne they serue, and then returne with wealth for King and Kingdome, and for those that set them foorth, in stead of Wood?

Answere.

E 2   Wee

Wee must with thankefulnesse acknowledge, though hee coldly set it downe, that our most gracious Soueraigne hath not by Proclamation onely helpt the Kingdome in that point, but with a prouidence beyond his Predecessors, besides his recommending bils in Parliament, and speaking eloquently for them, He hath vrged good husbandrie of Planting to vs all, the onely meanes to breede vp shipping Timber, since tall and goodly Trees doe neuer proue of Tillers, second springers out of olde decayed stockes, how well soeuer kept by statute husbandrie in Woods.

But was this Care (thinkes he) for Trees to looke vpon? The prouidence that bids vs go and plant, commands vs too to vse our wel-growne Timber ere it rot, as that would soonest that is fittest for great shipping. His Maiestie was loth to haue our Timber spent on Beggers nests (that growing scurfe vpon this Citie) new tenemēts, whose rotten rents make many Gentlemen before their time, or that our Woods should bee consumed in fire & Furnaces for glasses & such bables when God hath blest vs with a Fuell in the bowels of the earth, the wast whereof can doe no hurt: but as for building ships, his wisedome likes that well, and out of royall bountie, for incouragement giues them the most that build the greatest, A policie of his Princely Predecessors. If then these Eagles could foresee no inconuenience, what is he? that professeth himselfe

Able

of Trade. 29

Able out of sufficient testimonie (questionlesse) to affirme, that since the East India Trade, and mérely through their building and repayring of their Ships (their building though begunne but fiue yeares since) Timber is raysed in the Land fiue shillings in a load, nay almost not to bee had for monie. This makes the Companie flie into Ireland, And hee heard a skilfull Shipwright (doubtlesse) say, that all the Timber within fortie miles of London would not build such another shippe, as the Trades Increase, &c. *The seuenth Obiection.*

I Know what men in *Kent* esteeme of him, that said *Answere.* (because they agreed in time) that the building of *Tenderden* Steeple was the cause of *Goodwin* sands increasing: but if there be a man so neere of kind vnto a blocke, that hee thinkes cutting downe of Timber, Parricide: His tender conscience shall haue some more satisfaction.

It is no newes to heare the price of Timber rise, with most things else (perhaps through monies falling,) It did so, long before the *East India* Companie beganne, It doth so now within the Land, where neyther they nor any can build shippes: but to confound that poore Conceite, that they haue caused dearth, the *East India* Marchants Bookes will shew, that to this daie they haue in all of *English* Timber spent but fiue thousand, sixe hundred, twentie three loades, and one thousand, eight hundred, fortie two of plancks. Whereas I know of my particular acquaintances within his Shippewrights limits, the Companie are offered at this present more then that, at as cheape rates as when they built the *Trades Increase*:

E 3 And

And they that beſt can iudge the *Eaſt-India* Ship-wrights, ſent to bargaine for the Companie, auerre vpon their credits, that they know within that fortie miles, Timber enough to build not onely many a Trades-Increaſe, but to vſe their wordes, Ten times as many ſhips as the *Eaſt-India* Marchants haue.

Yet they foreſeeing ſtore can be no ſore, eſpecially neere home, and hearing how the ſtranger daily fet-ched away our Timber out of *Ireland*; out of an ho-neſt good affection to their Countrie, put their foot in there, and now prouide the moſt part of their ſhipping and materials ᵐ thence, in which they finde no ⁿ fault at all, ſaue (as he only truly ſaies) the charge and ha-zard: and if it ſhall ſeeme good vnto his Maieſtie to keepe our *Iriſh* Timber from the ſtranger, for to build Buſſes and fiſhing Veſſells for our ſelues; This ready Companie, to doe him ſeruice, and to good their Countrie, may perhaps finde meanes, to ſaue home-ſtore, by trying a concluſion in *Virginia*, which this worthy Author thinkes, men know not what to doe withall. Since therefore their prouiſion out of *Ire-land*, neither is for neede, nor to ſaue charges: What is he that requites that induſtrie of theirs, and hazard, with ill wordes?

Now Sir, wee are vpon his next Inuectiues, his maine battaile, nothing now but death of men, only a certaine looſe Wing, a ſtragling Obiection about ſhipping comes firſt in the way, and ſaies that

I know where in one Corner of a Countrie 2000. Tunne of Timber muſt be ſpent vpon one Marſh-worke, yet no man dreames of dearth.

ᵐ *They haue a ſtock of Tim-ber, Trees and Planke cut downe, and ſeaſoning there, and as the old is fet-ched away, ſtill new is prouided.*
ⁿ *I am ſure it is a great deale too ſer-uiceable for the ſtranger.*

The eight Obiection.

𝔗𝔥𝔢 𝔈𝔞ſ𝔱 𝔦𝔫𝔡𝔦𝔞 𝔐𝔞𝔯𝔠𝔥𝔞𝔫𝔱𝔰 𝔥𝔞𝔲𝔢 𝔟𝔬𝔲𝔤𝔥𝔱 𝔱𝔥𝔢 𝔟𝔢ſ𝔱 ſ𝔥𝔦𝔭𝔰 𝔬𝔲𝔱 𝔬𝔣 𝔬𝔱𝔥𝔢𝔯 𝔗𝔯𝔞𝔡𝔢𝔰, 𝔞𝔫𝔡 𝔭𝔩𝔲𝔪'𝔡 𝔢𝔲𝔢𝔫 ℭ𝔬𝔫ſ𝔱𝔞𝔫𝔱𝔦𝔫𝔬𝔭𝔩𝔢 𝔥𝔢𝔯 ſ𝔢𝔩𝔣𝔢, 𝔬𝔣 𝔥𝔢𝔯 𝔟𝔢ſ𝔱 ſ𝔥𝔦𝔭𝔭𝔦𝔫𝔤, 𝔩𝔦𝔨𝔢 𝔞 𝔅𝔦𝔯𝔡 𝔱𝔥𝔞𝔱 𝔪𝔞𝔨𝔢𝔰 𝔥𝔢𝔯 ſ𝔢𝔩𝔣𝔢 𝔤𝔞𝔶, &c.

But

of Trade.

BVt if the *Poet were aliue (from whom hee bor- *Answere.*
rowes that conceit) to reade first a Gentlemans *Horace, lib. 1. Epist. 3.*
Fishing-Proiect, and then this Trades increase, assuredly, His *Quæ moueat Cornicula risum, Furtiuis nudata coloribus,* in the proper sence, should not neede to force it selfe vpon the *East-India* ships: but to the matter of the Obiection; if he had his will, that the *East-India* Marchants might neither build nor buy: what had become of those old ships they bought, as the *Hector*, the *Ascension*, and the *Suzan*, of Turkie Marchants, and some others of other men? had they not lyen and rot for want of worke, or beene broke vp for fire-wood, as well as others since? Or would he rather that they had beene alienated into *Spaine* with the *Alceder*, a ship of foure hundred Tunne, the *Beuis* of *Southampton*, a ship of three hundred Tunne? or into *Italie* with the *Royall Marchant*, of foure hundred. The *May flower*, of three hundred. The *Prosperous*, of two hundred and threescore. The *Suzan-Parnell*, of two hundred and fiftie. The *Gold Noble*, of two hundred and fortie. The *Consent*, of two hundred and fourescore. The *Concord*, of two hundred and fiftie Tunne. Surely, an honest man would rather haue said somewhat of this sale, if hee must needes complaine, then quarrell that, which was but change with gaine vnto the Kingdome. Where then, good friend, in the Epistle is that *Candor animi*, in all Particulars? In all particulars it shewes it selfe alike, and euen as charitably in his following clamor, about losse of men: a subiect worthy of a little meditation.

It is a precious thing the life of man, and would to God our single Combatants, for idle wordes, would

wey

wey it well, at least those ioyes, that are expressed by the terme of Life to Come: Yet the true sweet thereof is not in length, but vse; a moneth of health more worth then yeares of sicknesse; an idle weeke not worth one houre well spent. And if wee looke vpon it, for it selfe or for our selues, to stay from Sea for feare of death, and starue at home, or pine away in pouerty, were foolish superstitious cowardize: But as wee are the Bodies of our King, and of our Countrie (though in truth their greatest treasure, witnesse a °*Pohatan*, or a ᵖ *Virginia*, without them yet.) This necessarie Relatiue of Soueraigntie. Liuing bodies, vnimploi'd, are nothing. And if vnhealthinesse or danger of mortalitie, should keepe vs from a course, wherein we may inrich vs, or our Masters, or serue the King, or good the Common-wealth: Who then shall liue in Rumnie-Marsh, or Holland, or our Cinque Ports, or Cities visited with sicknesse, or goe vnto the Warres? There is an Author that can make all these the price of bloud, with phrases: But perfect wisedome in all Common-wealths, hath honors, pay and priuiledges, to invite the priuate man into such dangers, for the publique good; And God hath giuen men wit and vnderstanding to finde out preseruatiues, as armor against euery perill, which In-bred courage, or obedience to Commanders, or care of those we must prouide for, makes vs vnder-goe. Besides, the common-wealth esteemes not of the life of any but good men, such as doe good, the rest are *Tacitus* his *Purgamenta Vrbium*, their death to her is nothing but an ease. Nay Mariners themselues admitting them to bee so scarce, were better die in the *East-Indies*, then here at home at Tybourne

° A poore naked King of
ᵖ The goodliest Countrie in the world, were it well inhabited.

of Trade.

Tybourne, or at *Wapping*, for want of meanes to liue; or else be forced to turne Sea-robbers, and (besides their other hurts) giue this mans *pen occasion to * 34. *pag* cast such shamefull and vnnaturall aspersions on our whole Nation. But I will spinne out this no farther: the paradoxe is needlesse; for the ground our Author tooke to fight this battaile on, will faile him. Vnskilfull Sericant-Maior, he is mistaken in his numbers. He saies,

𝔗hat by the losse of foure ships, we haue lost at least foure hundred and fiftie men: and in the Aduenture, of some three thousand, since that voyage began, wee haue lost many aboue two thousand. *The ninth obiection.*

BVt how many soeuer haue beene imploied since that Voyage began, vpon a true examination of our bookes, it doth appeare, that in all our ships that haue returned or beene lost, vnto this day, there were at first set forth but three and twentie hundred, thirtie and three men of all conditions, Captaines, Preachers, Chirurgians, Marchants, Nouices and all: so that, vnlesse multiplication helpe him, when those are reckoned that are out in very many Factories abroad, and those that did come home in 19. ships that haue returned safe, there will not rest much likelihood of many aboue two thousand cast away. As for his at least foure hundred and fiftie, lost in the foure ships, *Answere. Whereas hee speakes of Heathen mens bringing home our ships, it is a meere toy, for that they come as well to see our Country, and not neere so many as wee leaue for thē. The Cloue brought home the most, from Iapan, yet not the fift part of the ships companie.*

The {*Trades Increase* / *Vnion* / *Ascension* / *Suzan*} had but {211 / 70 / 70 / 84} {In al foure hundred thirtie and fiue, when they set forth.

F   And

The Defence

And three of these, the *Trades Increase*, the *Vnion*, and the *Ascension*, although the body of the ships were lost, as you haue heard, lost not thereby one man. But hee perhaps will mend this grosse account in the particulars. He saies,

The tenth obiection.

That Sir Henry Middleton carried out two hundred and twentie in the Trades Increase, all which liue Cargazon, ten only excepted, perished in that bloudy field Bantam, &c.

Answere.

BVt Sir *Henry Middleton* had but two hundred and eleuen at first; and notwithstanding the losse of his Monson, by his imprisonment, for all his afflictions, and the accidentall infection you heard of, besides foure that should haue beene executed for malefactors, that therefore ran away vnto the *Portingals*, and fiue that were drowned, and many that were slaine, when hee was so barbarously captiued by the *Turkes* at *Moha*, and sixteene that were left abroad in Factorie, there returned with Captaine *Best* thirteene more then the ten he speakes of. But he saies further,

The eleuenth obiection.

That Captaine Dounton, of seuentie which hee carried forth, brought home but twentie: the rest, their liues were sacrificed to that implacable East-India Neptune, &c.

Answere.

BVt Captaine *Dounton*, for all his dangers with Sir *Henry Middleton*, besides diuers left in Factorie, brought home twentie and seuen. But hee saies further,

That

of Trade.

That Captaine Saris and Captaine Towerson, whether through insufficiencie or no, he knowes not, but Captaine Towerson of 120. carried forth, lost 85. and Captaine Saris of ninetie and odde, brought home but two or three and twentie. And the Thomas was brought home by way of a wrecke, &c.

The twelfth objection.

FOr the sufficiencie of men aliue, able to answere for themselues, I will say nothing, let their actions speake. But for the reckoning, Captaine *Towerson* carried out but one hundred and twelue, of which he left diuers abroad in Factories, and brought home 35. And the Generall of that Voyage, Captaine *Saris*, that carried out but 87. *English*, and 4. *Indians*, did leaue at *Bantam* eight in Factorie, and fifteene in *Iapan*, and yet brought home many more *English* then he speakes of, besides three *Indians* for the foure that went out. Neither may one without a name, name the *Thomas* a wrecke, whose men brought shippe and goods into safe Port in *Ireland*, which if she had done sooner, as she might, and not striuen in the cold stormie winter, to come about for *London*, two moneths together, she had not lost so many men. But he saies further,

[marginal note: Captaine *Saru* would haue M. Pamphleter know, that he is not to learn the dutie of a Sea-commander from any of the wise Masters his Informers. He saies his voyage was the longest, and fardest, and costliest, and yet wealthiest of any returned hitherto, and that hee brought home aboue 40. men besides 15. Iaponeses for those left at *Iapan*, where he obtained certainly ample and honourable priuileges for our Nation.]

That by reason of the dogged starre of those Climates, of one hundred and eightie men carried forth by Captaine Best, there returned only thirtie, ouer and aboue foure or fiue and twentie left on the desperate account of the Countries Factoridge, &c.

The 13. objection.

BVt first, to satisfie this desperate account of Factors, you may know, that their returnes in euery shippe of ours, likely, many men, (ten at a time, and sometimes

sometimes more) sent out in other Voyages, which I doe neuer reckon, but onely giue a true account of those that did proceed in the same shippe. And so besides those which Captaine *Best* did leaue abroad in Factorie, he put eight into the *Darling*, (the Pinnace that attended on Sir *Henry Middleton*, and is now discouering in the *Indies*) and foure hee lost by his accidentall fight with the *Portingall*, and yet brought home sixtie and fiue. Who then can thinke this man had any minde to publish truth, that would not once conferre with Captaine *Best*, well knowne vnto him, as it seemeth by his friendly commendation, and one that could haue told him both the truth of our mens dying, and that the true cause (sauing ſ *Bantam*) is their owne disorder? Therefore

ſ This place is vnhealthie to our people, as time hath taught vs. So is *Scandarone* in the months of *Iune, Iulie,* and *August*, to those that goe into the Straights. We therefore change our Factorie from *Bantam*, where though some (as Captaine *Saris* 6. yeares) liue well, yet more haue died then in all our other Factories, if wee reckon not them that die of the &c. wome

Certainly neither the dogged starre of those Climates, nor that implacable *East-India Neptune*, nor that bloudie field *Bantam*, is so fatall, so mercilesse, so murderous, as the malice of this man, that to slander the *East-India* Voyage, hath kild many that came home in safetie, and some that were neuer there. But I resolued to giue you satisfaction, and not laugh at him. Know therfore, It is the Marchants griefe (and hee that knowes what hazard they doe runne, that haue their goods in Heathen Countries, in the hands of dying men, that must expect rich ships to come from places so remote, so weakly mand, thorow Seas of dangers, besides Pirates, will beleeue it is their griefe) vnspeakable, that hitherto they cannot absolutely cleare themselues from this (to them indeede great) mischiefe. For though they put their wealth into the
hands

hands of such as come by sute and friends into their seruice, though they giue them entertainment, and imprest for their prouisions, beyond all other Marchants; though they prouide what ere it cost, all that the wit of man, helpt by continuall experience, can inuent, for victuals, clothing, physicke, surgerie, to keepe them in good health, besides good Preachers, and the best Commanders, al that may be to preserue them: yet if (as for the most part through their owne abusing of themselues, with the hot drinkes and most infectious women of those Countries) they come vnto vntimely death, the Marchants, that by that meanes lose much of their goods, and hazard all, when they haue paid the friends or creditors not only all their due, but oft times giuen more out of charitie to such as want, shall yet haue such a man as this raise ghosts, rather then they shall not be haunted.

But by the blessing of Almightie God, now that we are acquainted better with that Voyage, and so taught to settle Factories in healthier places ; now that our Factors are more staid, and better knowne vnto vs, then many of those young men were that first aduentured on that then discouering Trade; now that our common Mariners, in effect the food of that mortalitie, (as may appeare by the often Voyages of our Captaines, Masters, Mates, and men of gouernment) shall neither be so long at Sea, nor stay longer on Land, then to vnlade and lade, and so return in fifteene or sixteene moneths, as in *Straights* Voyages; wee are in good hope that our ships will come as safe from losse of men, as the *Consent* did first, and Captaine *Newport* since, whose happie Voyages

F 3   taught

taught vs the experience. And so, Sir, our Pamphleter is now come *ad Triarios*, to his Reregard, his last Refuge, his owne Regiment, and that a ragged one.

Friends, Fathers, Widowes, Children, Kinsfolkes, and Creditors, out of poore Ratcleefe, Limehouse, Blackwall, Shadwel, Wapping, and other Sea-Townes, clamoring for the due of the dead, &c.

<small>The fourteenth objection.</small>

<small>Answere.</small>

I Would some other poore, yet honest businesse, could as well shake off this clamour, as the *East-India* purse doth, that giues such extraordinarie wages, and still paies so readily, that men for many moneths out in this Voyage, in continuall pay, although in their returne they chance to die, and leaue perhaps to the suruiuors their extraordinarie gaine by priuate Trade, yet the good money due soone dries the eies of friends and creditors, as it might doe widowes, but that the Marchants carefull chusing by their good willes none but single men, doth for the most part saue that labour. For my part, I that often visit [t] *Philpot Lane*, professe, I meet few sorrowfull *East India* Clients, but such as are refused to goe the Voyage.

<small>[t] Sir *Thomas Smiths* house, where the Companie entertaine and pay their men.</small>

And though I would not wish the *East-India* Marchants to answere this imaginarie clamour with setting truly downe how many Hogsheads of good Beefe and Porke, how many thousand weight of Biscuit they haue giuen to the poore, euen in the parishes and places which hee names; nor yet with telling what proportion weekely in pottage, beefe, and bread they send to the *Fleet*, *Ludgate*, *Newgate*, the two *Counters*, *Bedlem*, the *Marshalsea*, *Kings Bench*, *white Lion*, and *Counter* in *Southwarke*, besides good summes
of

of money yearely to releeue poore painfull Preachers of the Gospell, whose meanes are small, and charges great. For which and other workes of charitie, God hath so wonderfully blest their labours. Yet if they should awhile forbeare their almes, and let the poore soules know it is, because this man thus raild vpon them, thinke then but what an armie of cōplaints and curses would fall on him & all his fained rabble, which he brought to fight like Satans seeming souldiers in the aire.

Poore man, his case was desperate, and like the Captaine of the Fort that *Monluc* speakes of: he did but set vp old clothes stuft with straw, to winne a little time to runne away: for harke, hee is alreadie in his violent retrait, with

For certaine there is want of Trade. The Hollander would grow greater, if he had all this trade in his own hands: the Kings Customes are aduanced: this way Shipwrights are set a worke, &c.

And so forth with a *Misericordia*, till he leaue vs to examine the Baggage ——— Arguments remaining.

Inprimis, *Complaint of the Straights Marchant, &c.*
Dead alreadie.

Item, *The foundation of this trade was laid in the ruine of a Carricke taken by Sir Iames Lancaster, &c.* The fifteenth obiection.

Sore wounded, and not worth the knocking in the head.— Yet for full satisfaction, it was founded by Queene *Elizabeth* of famous memorie, before Sir Answere.

Iames

Iames Lancaster went to Sea: and that I may set downe her reasons in the Patent, for the honour of her Realme of *England*, for the increase of her Nauigation, for the aduancement of trade of marchandize, and for other important causes and reasons, &c. But alas, she wanted this mans wisdome to assist her Counsell, &c. What haue we next?

The sixteenth obiection. The iollitie of this trade proceeded from Sir Henry Middleton his trade comming out of the Mecha Fleet, whereby diuers Ships, as the Angell, durst not goe after into the Straights, &c.

Answere. First then, for iollitie of trade, the seuenth, the eighth, and the ninth Voyages at least, were gone to Sea before we heard one good word from the sixt, which was Sir *Henry Middletons*: and before returne of any goods, the tenth, the eleuenth, the twelfth were likewise gone, if not the thirteenth, with a resolution of the settled great Ioint stocke. The iollitie I thinke he enuies. Nor finde we fault with Captaine *Middleton*, although his Voyage proue one of our worst. But sure the Heathen man that said,

Tibi innocens sit, quisquis est pro te nocens,

will much condemne this man, that blemisheth, as much as in him lies, Sir *Henry Middletons* good seruice for our Country, to take the part of Heathen men, that haue more conscience, that complaine not, for they know the wrongs which they had done our Nation, and that Captaine, for whose valiant iustice sake they vse our people better euer since. As for the scare of

of Trade.

of some one ship, if it were true, wee wey it not, sith the whole bodie of the *Turkie* Companie, on good deliberation, were secure, as men that knew, Our *Lidgier* at *Constantinople* now shall find a readier eare to all Complaints since that example taught them, that our Nation can (as farre as 'tis) stoppe vp the mouth that giues them sweetest sustinance.

But, their commodities are vnnecessary, &c.   *The seuenteenth Obiection. Answere.*

HE meanes not this, I hope, by *Indico* and healthfull drugges, though *Callicoes*, and Silkes, and peraduenture Spice be censured. The truth is, in strict tearmes of need, our Land that flowes with foode and rayment may *Bee*, without all other Nations, but to *Bee Well*, to flourish and grow rich, wee must find vent for our abundance, and seeke to adorne vs out of others superfluities. So other Marchants bring in *Wines*, and *Sugars*, *Currons*, *Raisons*, *Oyles* and such like, that while we eat them, doe eat on vs, and so of manufactures wearing: But I shall shew you now a Mystery of the *East India* Marchants merit of the Commonwealth, euen out of their vnnecessary Wares.

In any of their Voyages, The Common-wealth payes nothing for the victuals nor the wages of the men, nor for the worke of Shippewrights, Smiths, Coopers, Ropemakers, Porters, Lighter-men, &c. and such like infinite number of Labourers which they haue continually in pay; but hath the imployment of all these, and the keeping of many Factors abroad, for the materials, out of which they rayse their shipping and prouisions, so that there rests to reckon vnto her,

G

The Defence

This stock in the greatest yeare, was but 36000. and The kingdome saues yearely in the price of Pepper, Cloues, Mace and Nutmegs- 70000. pounds besides alother wares.

her, onely the stocke of Marchandize and monie sent to barter.

This stocke in two yeares doth not rise vnto the summe of that which yearely since the *East India* Trade (as I shall shew you by and by) the Kingdome saues, in the price onely, of the Spice it spends, so that the Common-wealth hath more then two for one, euen in the first returne for her Aduenture. Now then marke further, ouer and aboue that which was left to serue the Land, from *Michaelmasse* 1 6 1 3. vnto *Christmasse* 1 6 1 4. There was exported of *East India* goods, out of the Kingdome.

As much In
- Pepper, as at two shillings the pound amounted to — 209623ˡ — 14ˢ — ᵈ
- Cloues, as at foure shillings the pound amounted to — 4338 — 16 — 0
- Nutmegs, as at two shillings eight pence the pound amounted to — 740 — 16 — 0
- Mace, as at six shillings the pound amounted to — 3613 — 4 — 0

In all 218316 — 10 — 0

So that by the *East India* Marchants happie charge and

of Trade.

and induſtrie, beſides the Cuſtome paid for it to the Crowne, and the imployment of many Shippes and Marriners, in ſending it abroad, into *Germanie*, and the *Netherlands*, *France*, *Spaine*, *Italy*, *Turkie*, and other places, there was alreadie in fifteene moneths, out of foure ſorts of Spice onely (not to ſpeake of the *Indico*, *Callicoes*, *China Silkes*, *Beniamin*, *Aloes-ſocotrina*, &c. then exported) aboue two hundred thouſand pounds ſterling, added to the ſtocke of the Common-wealth, to proceede for the inriching of the Kingdome in the nature of Cloth, Lead, Tinne, or any of our owne Staple Marchandize. Which I hope was no vnneceſſary commoditie.

But you that read may iudge by this what great Increaſe the Common-wealth will haue, now the Ioint ſtocke is ſetled, and are long, returnes by Gods grace, to be look't for yearly of many ſhips with many hundred thouſand pounds worth of Spice, *Indico*, *Callicoes*, *China* and *Perſia* Silkes both raw and wrought, and other Marchandize, to ſerue our ſelues, and moſt partes of the World as wee beginne alreadie, and ſhould more eaſily, if ſuch buſie men as this Pamphletor would let the Martchant doe it without noiſe. But

¶What haue wee the cheaper?

ILe ſhew you Sir, and ſince I ſo began, in Spices onely, which before our *India* Trade, were often accidentally ſold dearer much, but conſtantly, the loweſt price. *The eighteeth Obiection Anſwere*

The Defence

Pepper, was foure shillings the pound, at which rate, fifteene hundred bagges, containing foure hundred & fiftie thousand pouds, (the smallest quantitie, that the Kingdome yearely is esteemed to spend) amounted to ninetie thousand pounds sterling. But since our trade, the highest price is but two shillings the pound, so that the Kingdome saues in Pepper yearely halfe, that is — 45000l.00s.0d.

Cloues, was eight shillings the pound, at which rate, two hundred Hogsheads, cōtaining fiftie thousand pounds spent in the land) amounted to twentie thousand ponnds — But till the *Dutchmen* interrupted that part of our Trade, our greatest price was but foure shillings, so as the kingdome saued in Cloues — 10000l.00s.0d.

Mace, was ten shillings the pound, at which rate one hundred Hogsheads, cōtaining fifteene thousand pounds, the Kingdomes spending came to seuen thousand and fiue hundred pounds — But we haue alreadie brought the price to sixe shillings the pound, and so the Land, in Mace saues yearely — 3000l.00s.0d.

of Trade. 45

Of {Nutmegs, was fiue shillings the pound, at which rate, foure hundred Barrels, containing one hundred thousand pounds, our yearely spending amount to twentie & fiue thousand pounds, but by our price of two shillings and eight pence for a pound, the Kingdome saues.} 11666^l.13^s.4^d.

So that this Trade in onely Spice, doth yearely saue the Land―――――――――69666^l. 13^s. 4^d.

And if (as some perhaps for their particular aduantage of returning Spices out of *Holland*, would haue vs) we should trust vnto the *Dutch*, and leaue this Trading for our selues, how soone the price would rise, you shall perceiue by this particular Example.

About some two yeares since, our Marchants brought in a good quantitie of Cloues, which to ship out againe, they sold wet-dryed for two shillings and eight pence the pound, and the dryed for foure shillings: But by our next ships failing, we were forced to fetch from *Amsterdam*, where sodainely the Dutchmen tooke the aduantage, so that wee could not get (as all men know) the very wet-dryed sold by vs so lately for two shillings and eight pence, vnder seuen shillings sterling for a pound. Iudge then by this, how deare strangers would quickly make vs pay for all things, if we should giue this Traffique ouer. But,

Looke into the price of Victualls, how that riseth through their great prouissions, &c.   The nineteenth Obiection.

To

The Defence

Answere.

TO which I answere, that no sober man can doubt, but that the mouths the *East-India* Merchant sends to Sea, would eate at home: but further, hee that is acquainted with the finding and the feeding men at Sea, knowes well it would bee riches infinite vnto this Land, and vnto euery priuate Master of a Familie, if men would wast no more in victualls here at home, then Sea-men doe abroade, yet since hee sayes this is the poores complaint, in truth a poore one, it shall haue some further satisfaction.

The greatest fleet that euer yet the Companie set forth, was this last yeare 1614. the charge whereof amounted to one hundred thousand pounds.

In
- Shipping and their Furniture. 34000l.0s.0d.
- Victuals, imprest mony and other ordinarie and extraordinarie charges. 30000l.0s.0d.
- Natiue and forraine Marchandize, and readie mony, sent to Trade. 36000l.0s.0d.

More particularly this Cargazon of thirtie and sixe thousand pounds, was:

In
- Bayes, Kersies, and most broad clothes dyed and drest to the Kingdomes best aduantage. 14000l.0s.0d.
- Lead, Iron, and forraine marchandize. 10000l.0s.0d.
- Readie mony, in all the ships, but 12000l.0s.0d.

And

of Trade.

And it is worth the noting that this twelue thousand pounds, was scant one third part of that, which the Companie paid that yeare for the Kings custome, impost, and other duties, and not one third part of that which they paid Marriners for wages: but for the victuall, that is thus prouided.

The Bread of corne sent for of purpose out of France.

The Drinke, all in a manner Spanish Wines and Sider, little or no Beere.

The Flesh is Beefe and Porke, proportion'd into ship-messes, and that onely but for three dayes of seuen in the weeke, and but for twentie moneths of thirtie, the other ten moneths, which proues often more, is prouided in *India*, or parts abroad.

Now then, if our Obiector bee none of those, that rise vp early to follow drunkennesse, and continue vntill night, till the Wine doe inflame them, &c. if he be free from *Seneca* his *Fœdissimum patrimonioru exitium culnis*: if he be no *Fucus, & Piger, & Vorax*, no vnprofitable burdē, that cōsumes the good fruits of the earth, but labors not at all: yet in his best sobrietie and temperance, let him but consider his owne mouth, and he shall finde it iustlier to be blam'd for making victualls deare, then the prouision of the *East-India* voyage, and yet this mouth will not be stopt, but how. How now?

What Monsieur Transportation of Treasure in the Reare, among the baggage? with the Victualler of the Campe? You that heretofore haue serued so resolutely, before the King, before the Parliament, at the Councell Table; nay, almost euery Table, now dying in a Ditch? Alas

The twentieth Obiection.

The Defence

Answere.

ALas Sir, his deare brother in Armes Death of men, is runne away wounded to death by Captaine *Newport:* what would you haue him doe? When hee saw, that the *East-India* Companie, by the Bookes of Entrie with his Maiesties Officers, by their own books of Accompts, besides a sodaine and secret searching of their ships, had manifested that they neuer in any yeare (no not when they went to discouer what of our Commodities would vent in those parts) carryed were so much, as his Maiesties gracious Letters Patents doth permit. When he found that some particular Marchants of that Companie, did at one time bring into the Kingdome more siluer, then the whole Companie together did at any time carrie out. When hee perceiued, notwithstanding, that the *East-India* Marchant, to auoid all colour of scandall, did prouide, That forraine [u] coine, beyond the Seas, with much hazard (as lately at *Sandwich*) by bringing of it ouer in small Pinkes, and paying dearer for it, then others, yea, strangers here at home doe buy it to steale ouer for want of their licence. When hee beheld, to his great griefe, such daily increase of broad clothes dyed and drest, with other marchandize, and such decrease of readie money, in the Cargazon or stock they sent to Traffique. When last of all, he heard for certaine of a Factorie setled at *Iapan*, and of such store of siluer there, as is not onely like to serue the Trade in all those parts, but to returne perhaps some good part hither, what would you haue him doe, but hide his head? And yet you heare, he holds his manly words, he talkes of murmuring and *Charles* the Fifth.

But sure, men will not murmure, when they know
the

[u] It was euer the money of forraine Nations, which they exported, and that which Marchants brought in not our owne coyne.

* Out of *Halls* Chronicle.

of Trade.

the truth, and would thefe haftie Writers fill their braines a little better, ere they preffe them, by reading the Records of *Spaine* and *Portugall*, and better Stories then *Hals* Chronicle for *India* matters, they might finde reafons, to make more reckoning of the *Eaft-India* Traffique then th'Obiector doth; The fole fruition whereof hath yeelded many Millions yearely to thofe Nations, and as they fay themfelues was worth more to that Crowne, then the *Weft-Indies*. I am fure the fweet thereof was fuch euen in the Infancie, that x *Iohn* the Third of *Portugall*, gaue to that *Charles* the Fifth he mentions, before his going into *Italie*, three hundred and fiftie thoufand Duckats, onely not to interrupt his Peoples then beginning Trade with the *Moluccaes*: Which fumme of many a few Subiects in *Caftile*, did offer to repay (on ftrange eafie conditions) rather then their Emperour fhould fell the hope they had of wealth, from thofe rich countries.

x By an agreement made at Zaragofa 22. of Aprill, 1529

But I haue done, and now it may be mine Author, that in his firft Page, cald himfelfe, a Frefh-water Souldier, if he fhould chance to fee the Martiall order his Obiections haue appeared in, might beleeue himfelfe to bee fome great Commander, whereas the Truth is hee was but a Trumpet of Defiance to the *Eaft-India* Marchant, according therefore to his dutie, I would fend him back to take a view of all his Falfehoods, fcattered in the field, which I perfwade my felfe, will fhew him his ouerthrow was fhamefull.

At leaft, Sir *Thomas Smith*, iudge what it may bee, if fome able Marchant vnder-take the Argument, when fo much hath beene faid (and more that comes

H too

too neare matter of State, secret of Marchandize, hath beene omitted) by your faithfull Friend and Kinsman, that wisheth well to Trade and Marchants.

Dudly Digges.

Post-

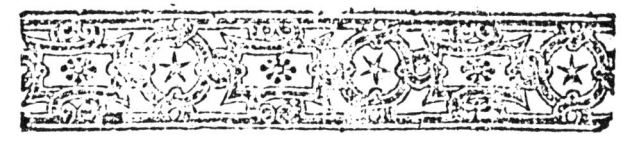

Post-script to the Reader.

Since hee that may dispose of mee, will haue these rough lines printed for your satisfaction, I that am neither ashamed of my loue to the East-India Trade, nor the truth I haue written, must (if but for fashion sake) say some what vnto you (   ) Reader. It may please you then to know, that the substance of this which you haue read, was taken out of Custome-bookes, out of the East-India Companies bookes, out of Grocers, Warehouse-keepers, Marchants bookes, and conference with men of best experience. As for errors of pen or presse, you will either not marke them, or can mend them; all I aske for my paines.

paines. *And so I leaue you, to commend (if you list)* piperi & scombris, *that* Trades Increase *to packe vp fish,* and *this* Defence of Trade *to wrappe vp spice : a couple of Inke-wasting toies indeed, that if my heartie wishes could haue wrought it, should haue seene no other light then the fire. So farre from the ambition of your acquaintance was*

D. D.

BRITAINES BUSSE,
OR
A COMPVTATION
aswell of the Charge of a Busse or Herring-Fishing Ship. As also of the
gaine and profit thereby.

With the States Proclamation Annexed
vnto the same, as concerning
Herring-Fishing.

By E. S.

LONDON,
Printed by William Iaggard for Nicholas Bourne, and
are to be sold at his shop at the South entry of
the Royal Exchange. 1615.

Britaines Busse.

Iuers Treatises haue bene published heere in England, some long since, some very lately, all of them inuiting to the building and employing of English Fishing shippes, such as our neighbour *Hollanders* call *Busses*, Principally to fish for *Herrings*, with which kinde of *Fish* (Almighty GOD of his rich bounty, blessed be his name therefore) hath abundantly stored his Maiesties Streames, on the coasts of *England, Scotland,* and *Ireland*, aboue all the knowne parts of the world.

Foure Bookes I haue seene of this Subiect.

One called the *Brittish Monarchy*, written An. Dom. 1576. which is nere 40 yeares past.

The second intituled *Hitchcocks New-yeares gift*, printed about 30 yeares since.

The third, named *Englands way to win wealth*, and to encrease Ships and Marriners, published within these 2. yeares, whose Author (I haue heard) was trained vppe from his youth : and very expert both in Nauigation and Fishing.

The fourth styled the *Trades Increase*, now newly come abroad.

Brittaines Busse.

In all which foure Bookes, but especially in the two last, the Necessity, Facility Profit, and Vse of that Fishing trade is proponed and handled.

After I had read three of the former Bookes, and before the fourth and last came to light, I was much affected with the businesse. And the more I consider it, the more is my affection confirmed and encreased. And out of vehement desire to see this worke, which I conceiue to tend so much to Gods glory: To the honour of our noble King: To the generall strength, safety, and commodity of all his Maiesties large Kingdomes and Dominions: And to the priuate and peculiar benefite and aduancement of euery priuate *Vndertaker* therein. I say out of vehement desire to see this worke in hand, & the prosperity thereof, I enquired as often (as conueniently I could) what Busses or Fishing Ships were in building on our Coasts, or were bought or vsed by any English.

At length I was informed (and that very truely) that one *Roger Godsalue* Esquire, of Bucknam Ferry in *Norfolke*, had begun to apply himselfe to this worthy work, and had on the Stockes at *Yarmoth* fiue Busses; whereof I vnderstand one is since that time launched, and that the other foure are in good forwardnesse. But when vpon enquiry after the Gentleman, I heard him to be a man of such vndoubted honesty and integrity, besides his other vertues and worth, Methought I did see God beginning this good businesse in a good hand.

Soone after I heard that another worthy gentleman, namely Sir *William Haruie* Knight had on the Stockes at Lyme-house in the yard of M. *Steuens*, Shipwright, another very faire large Busse neere as big as any Flemish Busse: which Busse I did after see my selfe when she was

in

Brittaines Buſſe.

in launching; and ſhe is now in the Thames before *Radcliffe.*

But beſide theſe two Gentlemen, I haue not yet heard of any Engliſh that haue yet applyed themſelues that way.

Now becauſe after many conſiderations of that matter, I perceiued that none of the foure Treatiſes before mentioned, had ſet downe in very plaine particulars the exact charge of Building, Manning, Victualling, and furniſhing of ſuch a Buſſe; and of the gaine or profite, which by Gods bleſſing in probability may redounde yearely to the particular Owner and Aduenturer of ſuch a Shippe.

And conceiuing Hope that the publication of ſuch particulars, might be ſome furtherance of the Action.

I reſolued to beſtow my beſt labours to get ſuch Particulars; and to that end I trauailed and conferred with ſuch both Ship-wrights, Marriners, Fiſhermen, Netmakers, and others, as I thought to bee able to informe me in the Premiſſes, that ſo I alſo might bring Straw or Morter to that noble Building. Or that I might picke or teaze Occam, or do ſomwhat, that am not able to do much.

And for that vpon conference with ſome experienced in this Herring Fiſhing, I am informed that a Buſſe of thirty fiue Laſt, that is, of ſeauenty Tunne, is of a very good and meete ſize or ſcantling, wherewith in a foure months fiſhing yearely to make the gaine or profite by Herring onely; Heereafter in particular ſet downe, beſides her imployment yearely alſo in Cod-fiſhing, &c.

A3   1

Brittaines Busse.

I haue therefore here imparted such Instructions as I could attaine vnto.

1. FIrst, of the precise dimentions or proportions of such a Busse of 35 Last. That is of 70 Tun.
2. Secondly, the vttermost Charges of such a Busse, and the particular of all her Mastes, Yardes, Sailes, Flagges, Pullies, Shiuers, Tackling, Cables and Anchors, together also with her cock-boat and oares.
3. Thirdly, the particulars of her Carpenters store, and of her Stewards store, and of her weapons, and the charge of them all.
4. Fourthly, the particulars of her Herring Nets, and of the VVarropes and other Ropes, Cords and lines, Corke, Pynbols or Buyes belonging to those Nets, with the particular charges of them all.
5. Fiftly, the particular Tooles and Implements vsed in dressing and packing of the saide Herrings, and their particular prizes.
6. Sixtly, the charge of one hundred Last of Herring Caskes or Barrels, and of Salt needefull for the packing of C. Last of Herrings.
7. Seuenthly, the particular charge of foure months victuals for 16 persons to serue in the saide Busse : and the particular charge of Physicke and Chirurgerie helpes for those xvi. persons.
8. Eightly, the particular vtmost wages of the saide xvi. persons for the saide foure months.
9. Lastly, the gaine or profit (by Gods blessing) hoped for, by such a foure months Herring-fishing.

After-

Brittaines Busse.

Afterwards is also set downe the yearely Charges of repayring the saide Busse: and of her apparrell and Furniture. And also of the said Nets, &c.

Together with the rest of the second yeares *Charge* and *Gaine*.

By which second yeares *Charge* and *Gaine*, you shall see the charge and gaine of euery year following so long as the Busse lasteth: which (*by Gods blessing and good vsage*) may well be twenty yeares at least.

HE that will giue a probable estimate of any Charge, must tye himselfe to some particular proportions, which hee must admit as the very iust allowances.

But I would haue none to imagine that I intend these particulars to be such as may not be varied.

If any be so vaine to make scornfull constructions, I hold such fellowes not worth the thinking on.

A Busse of 35 Last, that is of 70 Tunnes, must be on the Keele in length ——— 50 foot
And on the Maine beame ——— 17
And her Rake on the Stem forward ——— 16
And her Rake on the Sterne-post Eastward on ——— 7
And her wast from her lower edge of her Deckledges vnto her Ceelings ——— 13

Such a Busse with her Cabins, Cook-roome and other roomes fitted for the sea, and to this fishing seruice, together with her Ruther, Ironwork, bolts Chaine-bolts, Shroud-chaines, Nailes, &c. and her Cockboat and Oares will cost at most } li—s—d 260. li

All her masts and yards will cost at most ——— 8-0-0
The making and fitting her said masts and yards ——— 2-0-0
Her pullies and Shiuers at most ——— 2-0-0
Her rigging or Tackling ropes of the fittest sizes or scantlings, will come to at most 8 C. wai. of ropes which will cost at most 30 s a C. which comes to ——— 12-0-2

Her Maine-saile and two Bonnets must bee 11. yards deep and 16 cloaths broad of Ipswich Pole-dauis, which comes vnto 176 yardes of poledauis, which at ix d. a yard will cost ——— 6-12-0

Her Maine topsaile must be 8. yards deepe, and eight cloaths broad at the yarde, and sixteene cloathes broad at the Clewes, which takes 96. yards of Bungy Canuas, which at eight pence a yard will cost ——— 3-4-0

Her foresaile, the Course, & two Bonnets must be x. yards deepe and 12 cloaths broad, taking vp 120 yards of Ipswich Poledauis, which at ix.d. a yard comes to ——— 4-10-0

Her Mizen or Backsaile must be 4 cloaths broad and 5 yards deepe, which takes 20 yards of Bungy cloth, which at 8 d. a yard comes to ——— 0-13-4

So as all the Sailes take 420 yardes of Saile-cloth of both sorts, which 420 yards (at 28 yardes to a bolt) make almost 15 bolts of cloth. And the Sailemaker will haue for his work 5 s. a bolt which comes to ——— 3-15-0

Boltropes for all the saide Sailes. And Twine &c to make the saide Sailes withall, will cost at most ——— 1-15-8

——— 304 ——— 10 ——— 0

Two

	li.	s.	d
Two flagges or Fannes to obserue the winde by with their Staues, at ii. s. a piece	0	4	0
Two or three hand pikes of Ash at most	0	2	0
Two Waterskeits to wet the Sailes at xviii. d. a peece	0	3	0
Two Water-buckets at. vi. d.	0	1	0
Six Maps to clense the Busse vvithal, at vi. d	0	3	0
Compasses and boxes 2. at x s. a piece at most	1	0	0
Houre-glasses 3 or 4 at most at xviii, d	0	6	0
A Lanthorne for the poope	0	10	0
Two other lanthornes at xviii d. a piece	0	3	0
Fenders or long poles 4. at ii. s	0	8	0
Long Oares vi. at iii s. iiii d	1	0	0
An Iron Crow of 15 li. at iiii d	0	5	0

Cables. 4.
- One Cable of 9 Inches about, & C fadome, that is CC yardes long, will waigh about — xviii. C
- A second Cable 8 Inches ½ about, and of the length abouesaid will waigh about — xv. C.
- A third Cable 7 Inches ½ about, and of like length will weign — xi. C
- The fourth Cable 7 Inches about, & of like length, will weigh — x. C.

So all the foure Cables wil weigh about 54 C waight, which 54 C. waight of Cables at 30 s. C will cost — 81. 0. 0

Ancors 4
- One Anchor to waigh about — iiii. C
- A second to waigh about — iii. C ½
- A third to waight about — ii. C. ½
- A fourth to waigh about — ii C
- Foure Ancor stockes and the fitting of them at x s. a peece — ii l.

So all the 4. Ancors waighing xii C waight at xxvi s. viij d a C. will cost — xvi. li.

And so the 4 Anchors and their foure stockes will come to — 18 0 0

B   Ste-

Brittaines Buſſe.

	li.	s.	d.

Stewards ſtore.

	li.	s.	d.
Short Iron pothangers two at 12 d	0	2	0
pothookes 2 paire at x.d	0	1	8
A large Iron peaze pot of 5 or 6 Gallons	0	10	0
A large copper fiſh kettle about 32 li. wa. at xv.d per li.	2	0	0
A wodden ſcummer or two	0	0	4
Wodden Ladles 2 or 3	0	0	4
A Gridyron at moſt,	0	2	6
A frying pan	0	2	6
Pipkin two or three,	0	0	6
A Chafing diſh of Iron	0	2	0
A ſmall fire ſhouell and a paire of Tongs	0	2	6
A paire of Bellowes	0	0	8
Trayes 2 at xv d. a peece	0	2	6
Trugs 2 at ix d. a peece	0	1	6
Wodden platters 12 at iiii.d	0	4	0
Wodden Pottagers 24	0	2	0
Trenchers 4 dozen at iii.d	0	1	0
Baskets for Meſ-bread 6. at 4.d	0	2	0
Beere-cans bigger and leſſer 12	0	6	0
Taps and Fawcets 4 or 5.	0	0	2
wodden Butter-ſcales a paire	0	1	0
Leaden waights, 4 li — 2 li — 1 li — ½ li — q; li — at ii d	0	1	4
Tinder-boxes 2. furniſhed well	0	2	6
Candles at moſt for 16 weekes xxx li. at iiii d	0	10	0
Candleſtickes with Iron wyers 6. at 8 d	0	4	0
A Candlebox with locke and key at moſt	0	5	0

5————8————0.

Brittaines Busse.

	li.	s.	d
Carpenters store — Iron Esles to mend the Shrowd-chaines withal, if any should chance to breake—10 of 1 li. a peece at 4 d. a pound	0	3	4
Fids or Hammers two at 12 d	0	2	0
Orlup Nailes 3 C. at xvi d. a C.	0	4	0
Scupper-nailes ii C. at vi.d.	0	1	0
Spikes v li. at 4 d. a pound	0	1	8
Six peny nailes iii C	0	1	6
Foure peny nailes 3 C	0	1	0
pumpe nailes 3 C, at ii d. a C	0	0	6
A Sawe	0	3	0
Summe	0	18	0

Weapens, &c.			
Halfe pikes 10 at ii.s.	1	0	0
Muskets with Bandaleers, Rests and Molds 6	6	0	0
Gunpowder 6 li. at x d.	0	5	0
Leaden bullets 6 li. at iii d	0	1	6
	7	6	6

The Busse aforesaid must haue fifty Netts.

Nettes with the Appurtenances.

Each Net must be 30 yards, that is 15 fathom long vpon the rope.
Each net must also hang full and not stretched on the rope. Therefore each net before it come to be fastned to the rope (being stretched out) must be 35 yards long.
Each Net must be in depth 7 deepings.
Each deeping must be a fathom, that is two yards deepe.
So as each nette of 7 deepings, takes 7 times 35 yards of Lint or netting (of 60 Masks or mashes or holes deepe) which comes to iust 245 yards of Liut or netting of a fathom breadth or depth.
Which 345 yards of Lint or netting (ready made or knit) will cost iii d. a yarde, vvhich comes to for one net ——— 3 li. 1 s. 3 d. ————

li.	s.	d
3	1	3

Each net must haue a net-rope on the top of the net. So each net much haue 15 fathom of net-rope.
This net-rope must not be a stiffe tarred rope but lithe and gentle, and is best made of old ropes.
This 15. fathome of net rope for each net will cost, ii s. ————

0 2 0

Round about the head and two sides of each net (but not on the bottome) must bee set a small cord about the bignes of a Bow-string which is called head-roping or nostelling.
So each net takes 15 fathom, and 7 fathom and 7 fathom, vvhich comes to 29 fatnom of head-roping.
There is twenty fathome of this headroping in a pound waight of it. So each net takes almost a pound and ½ of this head roping, which is sold for 6 d. a pound. So the pound & ½ costeth,————

0 0 9.

Brit'aines Buſſe.

The 7 deepinges of each net are to be ſowed each to other altogether with a ſmall thred called *Twine Masking*. } 0-0-6.
Each net takes a pounde of this Twyne-maſking, which is ſold for————

Each net is to be faſtned to her ropes with ſhort peeces of Cords or lines of two foote long a peece called *Nozzels*.
Theſe *Nozzels* are tied very thicke, viz. at 4. maſhes or holes aſunder. So each net takes 150. Nozzels. } 0-1-0,
Theſe Nozzels are ſold ready cut out for viii.d. C. So 150 nozzels coſt————

Each net muſt haue a rope 5 or 6 Fathom long and an Inch through, that is 3 Inches and better about called a *Seazing* to faſten the net vnto the Warroape. This Rope will coſt iiii.d. a fathome. So for the ſaide ſix fathom———— } 0-2-0.

The ſeaming or ſowing together of the ſaide ſeuen deepings of each net, and the head roping of each net as aforeſaid, And the bringing of each net to the rope or ſetting on the Nozzels, Al this I ſay, is vſually done by a woman working it at 4.d. a day meat and drinke, or x d. a day at moſt finding her ſelfe, which woman will ſo diſpatch at leaſt two or three nets in a day. So each net ſo finiſhing, will coſt at moſt———— } 0-0-5s.

Euery net muſt be tanned in a Tanfat which will coſt at moſt———— } 0-0-10.

Nets,

Nets:
Warropes
&c.

All the said 50. Nets being finished must be hanged al a row vpon a strong large rope called a Warrope, which must be in bignesse 4. inches about.

This Warrope must be as long as all the said 50. Nets, that is fifty times 15. fathome long, that is, 750. fathome of Warrope.

So each Net taketh vp 15. fathome of Warrope.
An C. waight, that is, 112. li. of this rope is sold for at most 30. s. that is almost iiii. d. q; a pound.
An C. fathome of this rope will waigh neere CCCC. waight.
At which rate each fathome will waigh almost iiij. li. ½ which at iii. d. q; a pound will cost xiiij. d. ob. a fathome.
So for each Net 15 fathome at xiiij. d. ob. wil cost

	li.	s.	d
	0	18	2

Each Net must haue halfe a pound of Legorne Corke placed all along the Net at halfe a yard asunder: At which distance each Net takes 60. Corkes, or 60. halfe pounds of Corke, that is, 30. pound of Corke at ii. d. ob. a pound that is 23. s. 4. d. a C. will cost

| | 0 | 6 | 3 |

Those 60. Corkes must haue 60 Corke-bands to tye them to the Net: each Corkeband must be a fathome long.

These Corke-bands are made of the aforesaide head-roping line, whereof 20. fathomes waigh a pound as aforesaid.

So the said 60 fathomes will waigh 3. pound, which at vi. d. per pound wil cost

| | 0 | 1 | 6 |

For euery two Nets there must be a Pynboll or Bwy hooped, which will cost viii d. So to each Net allow for halfe a Pynboll or Bwy

| | 0 | 0 | 4 |

Each Pynboll or Bwy must haue a Rope of a yard long, to fasten it to the Warrope, which yard of rope will cost at most vi. d. So to each Net allow for halfe such a rope

| | 0 | 0 | 3 |

So it appeares by the particulars aforesaid, that each Net with Warropes and all other he appurtenances, will cost, 4, 15, 3.
And so the said 50 Nets at 4. 15. 3. a peece will cost in all

li.	s.	d.
238.	2.	6.

Britaines Buſſe.

		li.	s.	d.
Tooles and Implements uſed in ſhinge and packing of Herring.	Gipping or Gilling kniues 14 at 4 d.	0	8	0
	Roaring baskets or ſcuttles 24 at vi d	0	12	0
	Addeſſes for Coopers worke 6. at ii. s	0	12	0
	Drifts to beat downe hoops 12. at i d	0	1	0
	Irons to pull vp barrels heads 6. at 4 d	0	2	0
	Iron pipes to blow and trie Caskes, whether they be tight or no 3 at 8 d.	0	2	0
	Bended hoopes to ſupply ſuch as ſhall chance to breake or flye off, for an C Laſt, that is of 12 C barrels 24 C of hoopes at ii. s. a C	2	8	0
	Iron markes or letters to brand the barrels withal, viz. A B. for the beſt, S for the ſecond, W. for the worſt, at 8 d. a peece at moſt,	0	2	0
		4	7	0
Caske.	Herring barrels, an hundred Laſt, that is twelue hundred barrels, which containeth two and thirty Gallons a peece, will coſt fifteene ſhillings a Laſt, that is xv d. a peece, which commeth to	75	0	0
Salt.	A water Buſhell, that is 5 peckes of Spaniſh ſalt, will ſalt a barrell of Herrings. So to ſalt the ſaid C laſt, or 12 C. barels of Herrings, muſt be 12 C buſhels of ſalt, that is at 40. buſhels of ſalt to a waigh) iuſt 30 waigh of ſalt, ẃ at 40 s. a waigh, that is xii d. a buſhel, wil coſt	60	0	0

Memo-

Brittaines Busse.

Memorandum. A Flemish Busse doth often take seauen or eight Last of Herringes in a day. But if God giue a Busse one day with another but two last of Herringes a day, that is, twelue Last of Herrings in a weeke.

Then at that rate a Busse may take, dresse, and packe the said whole proportion of an C last of Herrings (*propounded to be hoped for*) in eight weekes and two daies.

And yet is heerein allowance made for victualles and wages for xvi. weekes, as after followeth.

Of which 16 weekes time if there be spent in rigging & furnishing the saide Busse to sea, and in sayling from her port to her fishing place; if these businesses I say spend two weekes of the time, and that other two weekes bee also spent in returning to her port after her fishing season and in vnrigging and laying vp the Busse. Then I say (of the xvi. weekes aboue allowed for) there wil bee xii. weekes to spend onely in fishing the Herring.

Victual

Brittaines Buſſe.

Victuall and Fuell for xvi. Men and Boyes, ſeruing in the Buſſe aforeſaid, for the Herring-fiſhing time, and the time of her ſetting out: and of her returne home, viz. from the 24 of May, vntill the 21. of September, which is 112. dayes, that is xvi. weekes, that is foure months.

		li. s. d
Beere.	TO allow for euery Man and Boy a gallon of Beere a day (which is the allowance made in the Kings ſhips) that is for the ſaide 16 perſons, 16 Gallons, that is iuſt halfe a Herring Barrell full a day, that is, for the whole voyage of xvi. weekes, or C xii. dayes, 56 ſuch barrels of Beere, Seuen of theſe herring barrels containe a Tun of Beere: ſo as the ſaide 56 herring barrelles full of beere, do make iuſt 8 Tun of beere, which at 40. s a Tun comes to—	16-0-0.
Bisket.	To alow for euery man and boy (as in hi.s maieſt. ſhips) a pound of Bisket a day, that is for euery man and boy for the ſaide 4 moneths or 112. daies, an C waight of bisket, that is for the ſaide 16 perſons, 16 C waight of bisket, which at 13 s 4 d. a C. will come to—	10-13-4
Oatmeale or Peaze	To allow amongſt the ſaid 16. perſons a gallon a day, that is halfe a pint a peece euery day, that is 112. gallons for them al, for the ſaid 112 daies or 4 months, which comes to iuſt 14 buſhelles, which at 4. s. a buſhell will coſt—	2-16-0
Bacon.	To alow alſo for each Man and boy 2 li. of Bacon for 4 meales in a weeke, that is for each perſon for the ſaid 16. weekes 32 li. that is 4 ſtone of bacon, and ſo for the ſaide xvi. perſons 64. ſtone of bacon, which at 2. s. 2 d. a ſtone, will come to—	6-18-8.
Freſhfiſh.	They may take daily out of the Sea, as much freſh-fiſh as they can eate,—	0-0-0.
Butter.	To allow euery Man and boy (to butter their fiſh or otherwiſe to eate as they like) a quarter of a pound of butter a day, that is, for each perſon 28 li. of butter, that is halfe a firkin of Suffolk butter, and ſo for the ſayd 16 men 8. firkins of butter at 20 s. the firkin—	8-0-0

44—8—0.

C

Cheeſe

Brittaines Busse.

Cheese. To allow euery of the said 16 men and boyes, halfe a pound of Holland Cheese a day, that is, for each persō 56 pound, that is, halfe a C. waight of Cheese. And so for the said 16. persons to allow viii.C.waight of Holland Cheese, which at ii.d.ob.the pound that is, 23 s.4.d. the hundred will cost —————————— li. s. d
 9 6 8

Vineger. To allow amongst the said 16. persons three pintes of Vinegar a day, that is for the said 112. dayes, 42 Gallons, that is a Teirce of Vinegar, which at vi.li. a Tunne Caske and all will cost — 1 0 0

Fuell. To allow for the dressing and boyling of their victuall viii.C. of Kentish Faggots, that is seauen Faggots a day, and 16. Faggots ouer in the whole time, which viii.C. of Faggots at viii.s. a C. coms to —————————— 3 4 0

——— 13 — 19 — 8 ———

Summe of all the said li. s. d.
4. months victuall is 57 18 8

I am informed that the Dutch Busses haue not halfe so much allowance of Victualles: But take almost al theirs out of the Sea

Phi.

Brittaines Busse.

		li.	s.	d
Phisick and Surgery helps	Sperma Ceti and a boxe for it	0	3	4
	Stone pitch and a boxe for it	—	1	4
	Aquauita 16 quarts is 4 gallons, at iii.s.	0	12	0
	Zant-oyle 16 pintes is 2 gallons, at vi s	0	12	0
	Honny, 16 pintes is 2 gallons, at v.s.	0	10	0
	Sugar 4 pound, at i s.	0	4	0
	Nutmegges a quarterne of a pound	0	1	0
	Ginger ½ a pound	0	0	6
	Pepper 16 oz. that is a pound	0	2	0
	Balsome and other Salues and old Linnen	0	10	0
	Syzers a paire	0	0	6
	A Steele Pleget to spread playsters	0	1	4
	A Chest with partitions for all these things	0	12	0
		3	10	0

Wages to the sixteen men	To a Maister for the said 4. months at v.li. a month that is, i.li, 5, s. 0 a week, or 4, s. ii. d. a day for 6 daies, or iii.s. 6 d ob, q; a day for seauē diaes.	20	0	0
	To two Mates at 24s, a month a peece	9	12	0
	To sixe other men at 20 s. a peece per month	24	0	0
	To sixe other men at 16 s, a peece per month	19	4	0
	To a boy at 6 s, a month	1	4	0
		74	0	0

Summe of all the Stocke and charge of one intire Busse, &c. the first yeare will be about — 934-5-8.

Brittaines Busse.
The difference or oddes between Charge & Aduenture.

IT appeares before in particulars, That a New Busse with her Nets and other appurtenances, together with all the first yeares Charge of Salt, Caske, Victuals, Wages, &c. will come to —————————————————————— 934-5-8

But it is to be obserued, that the owner & Aduenturer of such a Busse, shall not be out of purse, nor Aduenture so much money the said first yeare, by ——— 171—10—0

For the Wages aforesaide is neuer paide till the returne of the Ship or busse; which if it should neuer return (as God forbid) then is no wages paid So wages is parte of the Charge, but no part of the Aduenture And so the wages is spared from Aduenture, which comes to as before in particulars——————————————————————— 74-0-0.

Also it is to be obserued, that the busse can conueniently stow at once but 34 Last of Cask, which is but the thirde part of her said C. last of Caske in Charge, and so is also spared from Aduenture two third parts of her cask, which is 66. last of Caske, which at xv s comes to——— 49-10-0

Likewise the Busse cannot conueniently stow at once aboue tenne waighe of Salt, which is but a thirde part of her Salt in charge. And so is also spared from Aduenture ⅔ of her saide Salt, which is 20 waight of Salt, which at 40 s. a waight comes to——— 40-0-0.

Neither can the busse conueniently stow at once aboue her saide 8 Tunnes of beere in Charge. And so also is spared from Aduenture the one halfe of her saide beere, which is foure Tun, which at forty shillings a Tun comes to——— 8-0-0.

Totall spared from Aduenture ——— 171 li-10-0.
Which 171 li-10 s-0 being deducted out of the said Charge of 934-5-8. There resteth to bee aduentured the first yeare onely——— 762—15—8.

Britaines Buſſe.

The firſt yeares gayne in hope and likelyhood.

ABout a month after the Buſſes are gone out to ſea, a Yagar which is a Caruell or a Merchants ſhip (employed to ſeeke out the ſaid Herring-Buſſes, and to buy of them their Herrings vpon the firſt packing.) This Yagar I ſay (whereof are diuers ſo employed) comes to the ſayde Buſſe (amongſt others) and buyes all ſuch Herrings as ſhe hath barrelled (which barrels vppon the firſt packing are called Sticks.) And in part of payment for her ſaide Herring Stickes, deliuers ſuch Salt, Caſke, Hoopes, Nettes, Beere, and other Neceſſaries as the buſſe ſhal then want; (wherewith the ſaide Yagar comes alwayes furniſhed) the reſt the ſaid Yagar payes in ready mony to the Buſſeman. In this maner comes the Yagar to the buſſes two or three times or oftner in a Summer-Herring-fiſhing time. So as the ſayd Yagar buies of the ſaide Buſſe (if God giue them to the buſſe) all her ſaid C Laſt of herring Stickes. > 1000. li.

For which ſaid C.laſt of Herring-ſlickes, if the Yagar do pay but after the rate of x.li.a Laſt, that is xvi. s. viii.d. a barrell, then are the ſaide hundred laſt of Herringſticks ſold for iuſt ─────────

So (by the grace and bleſsing of God) the very firſt yeares herrings only, may bring in to the Aduenturer or owner all his whole both Stocke and Charges of ─934─5─8. aforeſaid. And alſo ─65─14─4─ ouer and aboue. And ſo the ſaid Aduenturer or Buſſe-maiſter, is like by Gods bleſsing, to gaine clearely the very firſt yeare.─────The Buſſe aforeſayde with all her apparrell and furniture, together with her Nets, &c. And ─065 li─14 s─4 d. in mony ouer and aboue, towards the vſe or Intreſt of the ſaid─762─15─8─ which the ſaide Aduenturer diſburſeth the firſt yeare out of Purſe,

Which is almoſt─9 li─0─0. in the hundred alſo for vſe.

C3　　　　　　　　　　　　The

Britaines Buſſe.

The ſecond yeares Charge.

	li.	s.	d.
Calking or carrying the said Buſſe yearely will coſt about	5	0	0
Repairing the Tacklings (which coſt at firſt xii li. as before)	6	0	0
Repairing the Sayles which coſt at firſt xx li, x s	10	0	0
Repairing the pullies, Shiuers, and other petty things about	1	0	0
Repairing the Cables (which coſt at firſt 81 li.) about	24	0	0
Towards the reparations of the Anchors (which coſt at firſt 18 li,) allow	3	0	0
Repairing the Carpenters ſtore (which coſt at firſt 15 s.) about	0	12	0
Repairing the Stewards ſtore (which coſt at firſt 5 li, 8 s. 0) about at moſt	2	8	10
Renewing ſhot and powder, and ſcowring the Muskets &c, about	0	0	0
Repairing of Nets with the appurtenances, with 50 new deepings, and a C fathome of War-rope, &c.	77	0	0
(Which coſt firſt as before in particulars, 238-2-6) the third part whereof is juſt 79-7-6.			
Renewing of Tooles to dreſſe and packe Herrings with all, (which coſt at firſt 4-5-0)	2	0	0
Renewing the whole C Laſt of Cask at xv s.	75	0	0
Renewing the whole 30 waighes of Salt at 40 s.	60	0	0
Renewing the whole proportion of victualles as foreſaid	57	18	8
Renewing part of the Phiſick and Surgery helpes (which coſt at firſt 3-10-0)	1	11	4
Wages as at the firſt	74	0	0

Summe

Brittaines Buſſe.

Sum.Tot.of the Charge of the ſecond years Herring Fiſhing will be as appeares about ——— li. s. d 400–0–0

But the ſecond yeares Aduenture and Disburſement, will be leſſe then the ſaide Charge,(as it was for the firſt yeare) by ——— 171.10,0

And ſo the Second yeares Aduenture will be onely about —— 228—10—0.

Towards which aduenture and Charge, there is before accompted to be gotten in money by the firſt yeares Herring fiſhing as before appeares —65—14—4.

So then the ſecond yeares Charge, beſides the ſayde 65—14—4. before gained, will be but 334—5—8.

But the ſaid ſecond yeares Aduenture,beſides the ſayde gaine, will be but 162—15—8.

So it appeares, That if the buſſe be onely imployed in fiſhing the Herring, and in that but onely one foure monthes in euery yeare: and that the Buſſe lye ſtill in her owne port all the reſt of the yeare: that is nine moneths in euerie yeare idle, yet ſhe gaines clearly euery yeare in that foure monthes (onely) the ſum of 600.li——0 s——0 d. If God giue her in that time,but the ſaid C.Laſt of Herrings, which being ſolde but at ten pound a Laſt,yeeld 1000.li.——0 s——0 d. Out of which deducting the ſaide ſecond yeares Charge of 400. li. aforeſaid,there reſteth as gained cleerely——600 li.——0——0 yearly by the ſaide Buſſe.

Memoran-

Brittaines Busse.

Memorandum, If the Aduenturer of such a Busse will also hire a Yagar by the Last, to take in his Herrings, and carry them into Danske Meluyn, Sweatbland, France, or elsewhere: Then the Charge and gaine of that course, will be as followeth, or thereabouts, viz.

YOu may hire a Caruill or other Merchants shippe for a Yagar to cary your Herings from the Busse into Dansk, Meluyn, &c. and to stay there for re-lading 14 or 20 daies, and then to bring backe to London such Wares or Merchandize as you shall there fraught her withall, for which fraught outward and stay there, and fraught home backe againe, the said ship wil haue at most—2—10—0 a last, that is 25 s. a Tun in and out. So the fraught of C Last of Herrings into Danske, and fraught of another C Last of Pitch, Hempe, Flax or Corne, &c. backe again to London will cost at most at—2 li—10 s—0 d. } li —s —d. 250-0-0.

Toll at Elsanor will cost out and in about————— 3-0-0.

I thinke no Custome is paide for Herringes in the East-country, yet suppose for Custome iiii s. a last, that is 4. d. a barrell, at which rate the C. Last of Stickes comes to——} 20-0-0.

For Cranage there allow at most 1 s. a Last, which for the said C last of Herrings is——————} -5-0-0.

For Wharfage there allow also after the rate of 12. d. a Last,————————} -5-0-0

For Warehouse-roome there till the Herrings be solde allow at most————} -2-0-0.

The repacking of the Herrings by the sworne Coopers of that place, and for new hooping 7 s Last of cask, which will be filled with the said C Last of Herring sticks, alowing 25. Last that is a fourth part of the C last to be shrunk away, that 75 last repacking and hooping at most at viii. s. a Last will cost——————} 30-0-0.

Sum:—315 l.—0 s—0 d. which neuer gots out of purse, but is paide when the Herrings are solde.

D

Brittaines Busse.

So if the saide C. Last of Herring so sent from the Busse to *Danske* do shrinke a fourth part, then will rest to be solde in *Danske*, *Meluyn*, &c. 75 Last of full re-packed Herrings, which 75. Last will bee there solde for at least 18 li. 12.s. 0.d. a Last, that is 31.s. a Barrell, which is iiii.s. i.d. a C. which is more then 2. Herrings and ½ a peny, by 7. Herringes in a hundred. And so the 72. Last of Herrings will be sold for ──

	li.	s.	d
	1395.	0.	0

Which is for the Herrings ── 1000 0 d
& for the fraught in & out, ── 315 0 d
And so is gained outwards only   80 0 d

Besides there may wel be gained by the return of 139. li. worth of corn or other Merchandize at least 120. more

Besides

Brittaines Busse.

Besides, the said Herring-fishing which is performed in foure months as aforesaide, the same Busse may be also employed the same yeare (presently after the said herring season) in fishing for *Cod* and *Ling*.

For the Herring fishing being begun yearly as before is shewed (about the 24. of May, and the Busse being returned home againe about the 21 of September, which is 16. weekes after: then the saide Busse and her men may rest in Port about 10. weekes, viz. from the 21. of September, vntill S. *Andrewes* tide, or the first of December after; and then set saile againe furnished with Hookes, Lines, Salt, caske, and all other things (heereafter particularly mentioned) needefull for the VVinter *Codfishing*, which may by Gods blessing bee dispatched and the Busse at home againe in her owne port by the first of March, which is thirteene weekes after, that is, in 91. dayes.

And so betweene the saide first of March and the 24. of May, which is iust eight weekes, the saide Busse may be carined or calked, and repaired and victualled & prouided of all things against the second or next years Herring-fishing. And so is the whole yeare ended & spent as aforesaide.

Brittaines Busse.

Now the Charges of the saide first Codfishing in the Busse aforesaide, with the 16 Men and Boyes aforesaid during the aforesaide time of 13. weekes or 91. daies will be as followeth, viz.

Tooles &
Imple-
ments.

Each man fishing for Codde and Ling, vseth at once 2 Kip-hooks, so 16 men may vse at once 32 of those hookes: but becaufe they lose their Hookes sometimes, therefore allow for euery of the men a dozen of hookes, that is 16 dozen of Kip-hooks, which at most wil cost 12 d. a dozen, that is, ─────────────────── } 0─16─0

Stringes for each Man sixe, that is, for the 16 men eight dozen of stringes, euery string must be fifty fathome long & about the bignesse of an Iackline, and it must be tanned. Euery such string will cost about 12 d. and so the said eight dozen of strings will cost ─────────── } 1─16─0

Chopstickes for euery man foure, is in all 64 Chopstickes. A Chopsticke is an Iron about the bignesse of a Curtaine Rod, and a yard long, and vpon this Iron is an hollow pipe of Leade 8 or 9. Inches long, and waighes about 4 pounde, and the Iron waighes about a pound, which Iron and leade will cost about 12 d. a peece, so 64. Chopstickes at 12 d. will cost────── } 3─4─0

For euery man two Garsangle-hookes. Totall two and thirtie Garsangle hookes. This Garsangle hooke is an Ashen-plant 6 or 8 Foote long with an Iron hooke like a Boat-hook at the end of it, one of these Garsangle hookes will cost 5 d. So the 32 Garsangle hookes will cost──── } 0─16─0

Foure

Britaines Buße.

Foure Heading kniues like Chopping kniues at xii.d.	0	4	0
Foure spliting kniues like mincing kniues at 12 d	0	4	0
Sixe gutting kniues at 4.d	0	2	0
A Grindstone and Trough	0	5	0
Whetstones two or three	0	3	0

Some of the old Herring Nets, to get Herringes to baite their Hooks. Or else to buy a Hogshead full of Lamprils which is the best baite for Cod and Ling. There is store of Lamprils to be had at *Woolwitch, Norwitch, and Hull*, which may cost about ——— 2 13 6

Baskets some of those before bought and vsed for the dressing of Herring and 12. other great Baskets at ii.s.6.d a peece ——— 1 10 0

——— 14 ——— 10 ——— 0 ———
D: *Caske.*

Brittaines Busse.

For barrelled Cod to prouide 35. Last of Barrels, which are the very same euery way, with the Herring barrels aforesaide, so the saide 35. Last of Caske, at xv.s. a Last, will cost 26.li.—5.s. As for the Linges (in hope) there is no Caske vsed for them, but they are onely salted and packed one vpon another in the ships hold. And if they take any Ling, then they must bring home the lesse Cod, and then also they saue some of the saide Caske——————————————

li, s. d
26-5—0.

Salt.

Each barrell of Cod will take a bushell of Salt vpon salt. So 35. Last of Cod aforesaide takes iust 420. Bushels of Salt vpon salt, that is, 10 waighes and a halfe of salt, which at 3.li. a waigh, that is 18.d. a bushell will cost——————————

31.10.0

Physicke and Chyrurgerie helpes.

To allowe as before is allowed for the Herring-fishing time, which (besides the Chest) will cost as before in particulars——————————

2-18-0.

Stew store Carp store

The Stewards store and Carpenters store aforsaid, will serue this voyage. So for them needeth no allowance——————————————

0-0-0.

60—13—0.

VICTVALL

Britaines Busse.

Victuall and Fuell for 16. Men and Boyes, to serue in the said Busse for the saide Codfishing time, and the time of setting out, and Returne home, viz. from about the first of December, vnto the first of March, which is iust 13. weekes, that is, 91 dayes.

Beere. TO allowe euery person a gallon of beere a day (as in the Kings ships) that is for the said 16 persons 16. gallons, that is iust halfe a Herring-barrell a day, that is for the whole voyage, 91. halfe barrels, that is almost 46, of those Herring barrels full of beere. Seuen of these herring barrels containe a Tun of beere: so as the said 46. barrels contain six Tun and a halfe of beere, which at 40. s. a Tun will cost ——— li. s. d 13-0-0.

Bisket. To allowe for euery person (as in his Maiest. ships) a pound of bisket a day, that is for all the saide 16. persons 112. li. that is an C. waight of Bisket a weeke, that is for the saide 13. weeks 13 C. of Bisket, which at xiii. s. —4.d— a C. will cost ——— 8-13-4.

Peaze. To alow for euery person halfe a pint of peaze a day (to bee watered and eaten with butter or else with bacon) that is a Gallon a day amongest them all, that is in all 91. gallons, that is 11 bushels and a pecke and a halfe of Peaze, which at 4. s. a bushell, will cost ——— 2-5-6.

Bacon. To allow for euery person 2. li. of Bacon a week for 4. meales in euery weeke, that is for the saide 16. persons 32. li. that is 4. stone of Bacon a week amongst them all, that is for the said 13. weeks, 52 stone of bacon, which at 2. s. 2. d. a stone, wil cost 5-12-8.

Freshfish. Fresh-fish they may take daily out of the Sea as much as they can eate ——— 0-0-0.

Butter

Brittaines Busse

Butter. To allow euery perfon a quarter of a pound a Butter a day, that is, 4 li. of Butter a day amongeſt them all. So for the ſaide 13. weekes or 91. dayes muſt be 364 li. of Butter, that is iuſt fix firkins and ½ of Suffolke Butter, which at xx.s. a firkin will coſt ——— } li. s. d 6-10-0.

Cheeſe. To allow euery perfon halfe a pound of Holland cheeſe a day, that is 8 li. a day among them all. So for the ſaid 13 weeks or 91 daies, 728 li. of cheeſe, that is 6 C ½ waight of Holland cheeſe w at 2 d.ob. a li. that is 1 li. 3 s. 4 d. C. will coſt } 7-11-8.

Vineger. To allow amongſt them all three pints of Vineger a day, that is, for the ſaide 91. daies almoſt 34. Gallons, allow a Teirce, which at 6 li. a Tun Caske and all, will coſt ——— } 1-0-0

Fuell. To allow alſo 8. Kentiſh Faggots a day, which for the ſaid 91 daies will come to 7. C. and a quarterne of Faggots, which at 8.s. a C. will coſt —— } 2.18.0

Sum of all the ſaide 13 weekes victuals and fuel, will come to as appeares ——— } li. s. d. 47. 11. 2 }

Brittaines Busse.

Wages. To a Maister for these 13. weekes at 5. li. a month, that is 25.s. a weeke a peece, is for both —— 16-5-0

To two Mates at 24.s. a moneth, that is vi.s. a week a peece, is for both —— 7-16-0

To six other men at 20.s. a peece per month, is 5.s. a weeke a peece —— 19-10-0

To six other men at 16.s. a peece per moneth, is 4.s. a weeke a peece —— 15-12-0

To the Boy at 6.s. a month, that is xviii.d. a weeke. — 0-19-6

60 —— 2 —— 6.

Sum of all the Charge of the first winters Cod-fishing, will bee as before in particulars about } 82-16-8

But heere is to be remembred that the wages is no part of the Aduenture (though it be part of the Charge. And so the Aduenturer shal be out of purse for this first Codfishing voyage, but only } li. s. d 122.14.2 at most.

Now if it please God in this voyage to afford vnto this Busse the filling of her said Cask, that is 35. Last of Cod only, that Cod will yeeld at least 20.s. a barreil, that is but 12.li. a Last: So the said 35 Last, will yeeld at least, 420.li —— 0 s —— 0 d.

Of the Lyuors of those 35. Last of fish, may well bee made 5. Tun of Traine oyle, worth at least 12.li. a Tun, that is but 12.d. a gallon, at which rate 5. Tun of oyle wil yeeld 60.li.

So by the blessing of God this Codfishing may bring in to the Aduenturer, as before in particulars —— } iust 480-0-0

Out of which 480.li. deduct the Charge abouesaid of 182-16-8, and then resteth to be cleered yearly by the said Cod-fishing —— } li. s. d 297-3 —— 4

And so it appeares that there may bee gained yearly by one Herring Fishing and one Cod Fishing in such a Busse yearly, the sum of 837-3-4. all Charges borne, and without any stocke after the first yeare } 897.li —— 3 s —— 4. d

F

Brittaines Busse.

BY that which is before set downe, it appeareth, that one Aduenturer or diuers Partners, buying or building and furnishing such a Busse, and aduenturing her to sea as aforesaid, shall disburse before and in the first Herring voyage, the sum of 762—15—8. out of purse.

And that the same 762—15—8. is clearly inned againe, together with all other charges, and 65—14—4. ouer and aboue within lesse then a yeare, & so the Busse with her Nets and furniture, and the saide 65—14—4. in money is gayned clearly the first voyage.

And that if the Busse do also that yeare make a Cod-fishing voyage as aforesaide, then I say, within the space of the said first yeare, the Aduenturer or the said Partners shal haue all their stocks into their purse againe as aforesaide, and shall also haue in purse gained cleerly the said first year 362—17—8 which gaine is more then is to be disbursed the second yeare in repayring the said Busse, with her appurtenances, &c. And also in furnishing her with new Herring Cask, Salt, Victual, &c. for the second yeares Herring fishing.

And that the said Aduenturer or Partners, after the saide first yeare, shall neuer be out of purse any money at all.

But that the first yeares cleare gaine will stocke him or them so sufficiently for the vse of this Busse, as by the same they may get cleerely after the saide first yeare, by two such voyages in that busse, yearly ouer and aboue all charges.

$$\left\{ \begin{array}{c} \text{—li.—s.—d.} \\ \text{—897-3—4.} \end{array} \right.$$

And that if the said Aduenturer or Partners will make but onely one Herring voyage yearely, then by that one onely Herring voyage yearely, the saide busse may get cleerely *per annum*, as is before declared.

$$\left\{ \begin{array}{c} \text{—600—0—0} \\ \text{Ouer and aboue all charges.} \end{array} \right.$$

I

Brittaines Busse.

I Confesse the priuate gaine to euery Vndertaker before propounded, may seeme too great to be hoped for: but before any conclude so let them read the Proclamation concerning this businesse, made by those thriuing States of the vnited prouinces of the Low Countries, and let them consider what should mooue those States in that publique proclamation, to call this Herring fishing, the *Chiefest-Trade*, and *Principall Gold-Mine* of those vnited prouinces, and to shew such *Iealousie*, and prouide so very carefully for the preseruation thereof, *If the gaine thereby were not exceeding great and extraordinary*.

That Proclamation translated out of Dutch into English, is affixed to the end of the Booke before mentioned, called *Englands way to win wealth*: and is here also againe annexed to these presents, as a thing to be often seene and considered of vs.

And for my selfe, I say that I know, that *No man may doe euill, that good may come of it*: Therefore I would not deuise a lye to perswade any to a worke how good soeuer; nor commend that to others, which my owne heart were not first strongly perswaded to be commendable: yet as I denye not but that I may erre in some of so many particulars: so I disdaine not, but rather desire to see such errors, honestly and fairely corrected by any that out of more skill, and desire of perfecting and furthering this good worke, shall finde out any such errors.

And whether this Fishery be *Necessary* for this *Commonwealth* or no, let the present condition and estate of our shipping and Mariners, and Sea Townes, and Coastes, which (as the meanes) should be the wals and strength of this Ilandish Monarchy; I say let them speake. I will say no more to this poynt, as well for other reasons, as also because this matter is but for a fewe alas: namely for those onely that preferre the Common wealth to their owne priuate: and they are wise, and a word is enough to such.

If any be so weake to thinke this Mechanicall Fisher-Trade not feasible by the English people: to them I may say with *Salomon* Goe to the Pismire looke vpon the Dutch thou sluggard, learne of them, they do it daily in the sight of all men at our owne doores, vpon our owne coastes. But some will needs feare a Lion in euerie way, because they will imploy their Tallents no way, but lie vnprofitablie at home alwaies.

E 2

Brittaines Busse.

The difficulties that Vnwillingnes hath obiected, Consists in want of Men, of Nets, of Caske, of Timber, and Plank, of Vtterance or Sale, and of the feare of Pyrats, of euerie of which a word or two.

THE 16. Men and boyes before admitted to serue in the saide Busse, may bee these: (viz.) A Mayster, a Mate, foure ordinary Sailors, and foure Fisher-men, there is ten, and then six Land-men and boyes to bee trained vp by the former Ten men in the *Art of Sayling,* and Craft of *Fishery.*

By which meanes euery Busse shall be a Seminary of Saylors and Fishers also, for so shall euery busse breede and make sixe new Marriners: and so euery 100. busses breede 600. new marriners to serue in such other busses as shall be after builded, which is also no small addition to the strength of this state.

Marri- ners.   Now if there were 100. busses presently to bee buil- ded, I would make no doubt (as hard as the world goes) but before they could be fitted for the Sea, there may be gathered vp about the Coast-Townes of his maiesties Dominions at least an C. able Maisters to take Charge of them. And another C. of Marriners to goe with them as their Mates: and foure C. Saylors to serue vn- der the saide C. Maisters, that is in all but 600. Marri- ners and Saylors. For I finde in the 35. page of *Englands way to win wealth* (the Author whereof was a *Yarmouth* man) that the last winter but one, *There were in that one Towne of Yarmouth* 300. *idle men that could get nothing to do, liuing poore for lacke of employment, vvho most gladly vvould haue gone to Sea in Pinkes, if there had beene any for them to goe in.* I haue reported his owne words.

And

Britaines Buße

Fisher-men.

And for the foure hundred Fishermen to serue in the C. Busses, they would soone be furnished out of those poore Fishers in Small boates, as *Trau'es, Cobbles, &c.* which fish all about the Coastes, which poore men by those small vessels can hardly get their bread, and therefore would holde it great preferment to bee called into such Busses where they may haue meat, drinke, and wages as before is liberally propounded for such. Besides, which if neede be there are too too many of those pernitious *Trinker-men*, who with Trinker-boates destroye the Riuer of Thames, by killing the Fry and small Fish there, euen all that comes to Net, before it bee eyther meate or Marketable. Which Trinkermen (if they will not offer themselues) may by order and authority of our State be compelled to giue ouer that Euil, and to follow this good Trade.

Landmẽ for a Seminary.

But for the saide 6.C. Land-men to serue in these C Busses we neede not study where to finde them; if such shoulde not seeke for seruice in these Busses, the verie streets of London and the Subburbs will soone shew & afford them, if it were so many thousand I thinke. Idle Vagrants so extreamely swarme there as all knowe. So much for men.

Nets.

Nettes will be the hardest matter to prouide at the first; yet I vnderstand that the before named Knight, Sir *William Haruey*, had in few weekes or moneths prouided all his Nets for his great Busse. And my selfe was offered Nettes for halfe a dozen Busses, if I would haue had them the last Sommer: and if there were now 100. Busses in building, I am informed of one that will vndertake to furnish them all with Nets. And after these Busses shall once be seene, many for their owne gaine will prouide for Hemp, twine, & all necessaries to the making of

E 3   Nets

Brit'aines Buſſe.

Nets enough. And doubtles *Scotland* and *Ireland* will preſently afford good helpe in this behalfe.

Caske.   Caske will be plentifully ſerued by *Scotland* and *Ireland*, though we ſhould make none of Engliſh Timber.

Timber & Plank.   And for all the great and pittifull waſte of our Engliſh Woods, yet will England afford Timber & Plank enough for many Buſſes: but (to ſpare England a while) *Ireland* will yeeld vs Buſſes enough beſides many other good Shippes, if need be; and *Scotland* will help vs with Maſts, but if we would ſpare ſo neare home, we may help our ſelues out of *Virginia* and *Sommer-Iſlands*. I wis the Dutch who haue no Materials in any Dominions of their owne, haue made harder and deerer ſhifts for their multitudes of Ships of all ſorts: If they had ſhifted off the building of Ships, becauſe they had no Timber or other ſhipping ſtuffe of their owne in their owne Lands, what a poore, naked, ſeruile people, had that free people beene ere this day?

Vtterāce or Sale.   Touching Vtterance and Sale of Herrings when we ſhall haue them: I am informed that there is yearely vttered and ſpent in his Maieſties owne Dominions, at leaſt ten thouſand Laſt of Herrings, which being ſerued by our ſelues, will keep in the Land aboundance of Treſure, which the Dutch yearely carry out for the Herrings which they catch on our own coaſts, and ſell to vs. Now, if ſuch a Buſſe as aforeſaide get yearely C. Laſt of Herrings, as aforeſaid: then an hundred Buſſes taking yearely C. Laſt a peece, doe take in all ten thouſand Laſt of Herrings. So then his Maieſties owne Dominions wil vtter all the Herrings which C. Buſſes ſhal take in a year. And then if wee ſhall haue 500. Buſſes more, I am perſwaded we may in *France*, and in *Danske*, & in other forraigne parts, haue as good and ready ſale for them, as the Dutch

Britaines Busse.

Dutch haue for theirs; for I heare that the Dutch could yearely vtter double so many as they doe sell if they had them. But if that should not bee so, surely it were too great pouerty for English mindes (like Horses that know not their owne strength) to feare to set foote by the Dutch, or by any other people vnder Heauen, or to feare to speede woorse in any Market or place then they: and yet not be driuen to beat down the Markets neither, except the Dutch should prooue more froward and fond then I can yet mistrust: but if they should, I will not bee perswaded to thinke, but that the worser part would fall out to their share at last.

If there will bee imployment but for 1000. Busses, me thinke they should thanke vs, (as for many other benefits, so for this,) that wee will bee contented that they share with vs, by vsing onely 500. Busses, & to fish frendly in consort, as it were with other 500. Busses of ours. But if they should alleadge, that they now hauing a thousand, shall haue (in that case) imployment for the other 500: why then perhappes wee may in friendly manner cope with them, and buy of them the other 500. of the said Busses.

I thanke God I neither hate nor enuy the Dutch; nay (for good and due respects) I preferre them to all other forraigne Nations in my loue; and they acknowledging vs as they ought, wee shall I hope doe them no wrong, and they must doe vs right.

I haue herein bin longer then I meant, onely because there came euen now to my minde some reports that I haue heard, (but doe not beleeue) of very foule and insolent dealing of their Busse-men with our poore weake Fisher-men vppon our Coastes. But if it were true, as I doubt it at least; yet I would not hate nor speak euill of

a

Brittaines Buſſe.

a whole State for the ſawcie preſumptions of a particular man, or of a few men, and thoſe perhappes prouoked thereto, by our owne Double-Beere of England.

Pirats & Enemies. It is too true that all ſeas are too full of Pirats, and that amongſt them (which wee haue great cauſe to lament) our Engliſh abound, who are too ready to iuſtifie their lewd errors with the want of imployment. It is true alſo, that men are not to get their liuing by ſinful violent, and vnlawfull courſes; yet I would they were ſtript of that colour and pretence, (which a good fleete of Buſſes would doe:) Beſide, ſuch a fleet of Buſſes will (by Gods grace be ſoone able to maintaine about them a guard of ſtrong warlike ſhips wel appointed to defend them. And in time of neede alſo to ſerue his Maieſty, and offend his enemies: and ſuch a guard will be very requiſite, althogh God hath ſo laid and placed the Herrings, as our Buſſes ſhall ſeldome need to lie or to labour out of the light of our owne ſhores. So much of the facility.

Laſtly, touching the vſe of this famous Fiſher-trade, I will onely commend vnto your conſiderations, that which is written thereof in all the foure Bookes before mentioned: namely, in the *Brittiſh Monarchy*, and *Hitchcocks New-yeares-guift*, and in *Englands way to win wealth &c.* and in the *Trades increaſe.* The Dutch haue thereby as by their onely or chiefe meanes curbed and bearded their aduerſaries; what then may wee doe by it, if God pleaſe, we I ſay to whome he hath vouchſafed multitudes of other helpes (which Dutch land hath not) to ſecond this; this trade ſets awarke all their idle, it keeps their gold & ſiluer in their dominions and multiplies it.

And I ſee not why the ſame trade ſhould not bee of the ſame vſe to vs.

Now

Brittaines Busse.

1. NOw Aboord our Busses again, which once wel established and followed, will in short time I hope by Gods blessing set many Ploughmen heere on worke, to sowe Hemp & Flax, both in *England, Scotland & Ireland*.

2. And wil conuert our Idle bellies, our Beggers, our vagabonds and Sharkes into lusty *Hempbeaters, spinners, Carders, Rope-makers, Net-makers, Coopers, Smiths, Shipwrights, Calkers, Sawyers, Saylers, Fishermen, Bisket-bakers, weauers of Pole-dauis, Sayle-makers*, and other good labouring Members.

3. And will more warrant and incourage our Magistrates to punnish the Idle, the sturdy begger, and the Theefe, when these Busses shall finde imployment for them that wil worke.

4. And will be a meanes that the True, poore, aged, and impotent shal be better and more plentifully, yet more easily and with lesse charges releeued, when onely such shall stand at deuotion, and no valiant Rogues shall share in the Almes of the charitable as now they do.

5. And will helpe to bring euery one to eate their own bread.

6. Yea, and will supply his Maiest. Armies and Garrisons in time of neede with many lusty able men insteede of our Bare-breeched Beggers and nasty Sharkes, that are as vnskilfull and as vnwilling to fight as to worke.

7. And will keepe and bring in abundance of Gold and Siluer.

I know and confesse that it is not in Man to promise these or any of them peremptorily, but all these are the euident effects of this Fishery amongst the Dutch.

And therefore I may conclude, That we are to hope for like blessing, by our like lawfull and honest endeuors in this trade of fishery which almighty God hath brought home to our doores to imploy vs in, whereby he also giues vs a comfortable calling to the worke.

Brittaines Busse.

TO begin withall, if but some of our Noblemen, and some of our Gentry, and some Cittizens and others of ability, each man for himselfe, would speedily prouide and imploy at least one Busse a peece, so as some good store of Busses may (amongest them in that manner bee speedily prouided and imployed, to ioyne with Sir *William Haruey*, who is already entred the field alone. No doubt but his Maiesty will bee pleased (at their humble suite) to encourage and incorporate them with priuileges, immunities, and authority; and so they may choose amongst themselues, some meet officers and ouerseers, and make meete lawes and orders for the due and seasonable taking, curing, packing, and selling of the saide Herrings, &c. As the French and Straights Merchants who being so incorporated, yet haue euery man his own ship, or the ship hee hiers: and each man by himselfe or by his Factor, goes out, returnes, buyes & sels, not transgressing the priuate lawes and orders of their respectiue companies.

But if at the first entrance there will not bee any competent number of Busses so prouided, and Aduentured as abouesaid. If his Maiesty will be pleased so to incorporate some fit for this worke; and (out of that corporation) a sufficient Treasurer, and other needefull officers be here chosen & made known; then may all that please, (of whatsoeuer honest condition) bring in (by a day to be assigned) what sum of money any shal like to Aduenture herein, from 5. pounds vpwards.

And when there shall be brought in 70. or 80. thousand pounds, then presently the said Officers to prouide an hundred Busses, which with that money will be royally built and furnished, and all their first yeares charge

And

Frittaines Busse.

And as more stocke shal come in, so also more Busses to be so prouided and added to those former, &c. All which may bee (as in the now East India company) the ioynt stocke and Busses of the company.

Of which Ioynt stocke and Busses, euery aduenturer according to the proportion of his said Aduenture, may yearely know, giue, and receiue his proportion, as it shal please God to dispose of the whole fleete and businesse. But whereas in the said East India company, and others such like, as haue a common Treasury, whereinto euery Aduenture is promiscuously put, the saide Aduentures once brought in, are there still continued in banke, and often additions cald for. In this Fishing company, euery Aduenturer shall but onely (as it were) lend the mony he aduentureth for one yeare or there abouts, as before is shewed.

Now for the good gouernment and sincere disposition of this Ioynt stocke, &c. It would be specially prouided (amongest other ordinances and prouisions) that all Officers be only annuall; and that those be freely chosen and yearely changed by the more voats of the company, yearely to be assembled for that purpose. And that whatsoeuer gratuities, or rewards, or fees, shall be yearly giuen to such Officers, may (not onely in grosse, but) in particular be distributed or set down by the more part of voyces of the company so assembled; and not one grosse sum giuen, bee deuided or distributed by any one man: for so may the company with their owne money arme and enable one man, (first thereby made proud) to ouer-rule and keep vnder themselues, by binding his fellow officers to himselfe, to the neglect of the generality, whose proper gifts they be, though by that ill meanes it be not acknowledged, besides many other mischiefes &

F 2   in-

Brittaines Busse.

inconueniences, which may come by the ouerweening of one or fewe men, whilest others of better deserts perhaps are neglected and not looked on, to the mouing of much offence, murmur, and enuy in some; and of pride, insolency and arrogancy in others.

By this last mentioned promiscuous course of Ioynt-stocke, after the rate of Aduenture and charge & gaine, before in particulars set downe, it appeares: That

Euery Aduenturer of C li. may gaine clearly *per annum*. —— 75—0—0
Euery Aduenturer of xl li. may gaine clearly *per annum* —30—0—0
Euery Aduenturer of xx li may gaine clearly *per annum*. —— 15—0—0
& euery Aduenturer of v. li. may gaine clearly *per annum*: —— 3—15—0

Surely I hope this famous Citty (euer forward for the kingdomes good) will for their part prouide and furnish the first C. of Busses at the least, and thereby according to their former noble examples, (as the cresset of the kingdome) giue light to the rest of the land to follow them by.

And I thinke the East India company will liberally further this worke: for that thereby some of their greatest wants are like to be supplied.

I speake as I thinke without insinuation, which I hate as much as rayling.

And I neither hope for, nor desire any other gaine hereby, then my share in the common good that all this land shall by Gods blessing reape by this businesse, and the proportionable gaine of mine Aduenture therein.

THE

THE
States Proclamation tranfla-
ted out of *Dutch*.

THE States generall of the Vnited Prouinces of the Low countries vnto al thofe that fhall fee or heare thefe prefents greeting. Wee let to weet, that whereas it is well knowne, that the great fifhing and catching of Herrings, is the chiefeft Trade and principal Gold-mine of thefe Vnited Countries, vvhereby many thoufands of Houfhoids, Families, Handi-crafts trades and Occupations are fet on worke, well maintained and profper, efpecially the Sailing and Nauigation, as vvell within as without thefe Countries, is kept in great eftion. Moreouer, many Returnes of Money, with the encreafe of the Meanes, Conuoyes, Cuftomes, & Reuennues of thefe Countries are augmented thereby and profper: and forafmuch as there is made from time to time many good Orders, concerning the catching, falting, and beneficiall vttering of the faid Herrings to the end, to preferue and maintaine the faid chiefe Trade in the Vnited Prouinces; which Trade, by diuers encounters of fome that feeke their owne Gaine, is enuyed, in refpect of the great good it bringeth to the vnited countries. And VVee are informed, that a newe deuice is put in practife to the preiudice of the Trade, to Tranf-
port

port out of the Vnited Countries into other countryes, Staues for Herring-barrels made heere, and halfe Herring-barrels, put into other Barrels and Nets, to crosse the good Orders and Policy heere intended to them of these Countries, for the catching, salting, and selling the Herrings, dressed in other countries, after the order of these Countries, whereby this chiefe Trade should bee decayed heere, and the Inhabitants of these Countryes damnified, if that we make not prouision in time against such practises. Therefore Wee, after mature Iudgement and deliberation, haue forbidden and interdicted, and by these Presents doe forbid and interdict, all, and euery one, as well Home-borne and Inhabitantes, as strangers frequenting these parts, to take vp any Herring-barrels, or halfe ones prepared, or any kind of nets in any Ship, Towne, or Hauen of the vnited Prouinces, to be sent into other Countries or Places, vpon paine of confiscation of the same, and the ship also wherein they shalbe found, besides a penalty of 200. of Netherlandish siluer Royals for the first time, and for the second time aboue confiscation of Ship and Goods, and 400. of the saide Royals of siluer, and for the third time, aboue confiscation of ship and goods, and 600. of the saide Royals of siluer and corporall punishment: all which confiscations and penalties shall be distributed, one third part to the profit of the Plaintife, one third part to the poor, and one third part to the Officers where the saide confiscation shall be demanded: and not onely they shal incurre this penalty, which after shall be taken with the deed, but they also, that within one yeare after the deed shall bee convicted: and that none may pretend ignorance, and that this order may be in all places duely obserued, and the offenders punished according to iustice:

We

Wee will and require, our deere and well-beloued Eſtates, Gouernors, Deputies of the councell, and the Eſtates of the reſpectiue Prouinces of *Gilderland*, and the county of *Satfill* in *Holland*, *Weſt-Freeſland*, *Zeland*, *Ytricts*, *Freeſland*, *Merizel*, the Towne of *Groyning*, and the circumiacent places: and to all Iuſtices and officers, that they cauſe to be publiſhed in all places, and proclaimed where the vſuall Proclamation and Publication is made: VVe do charge alſo the Chancellors and Prouinciall councell, and the councell of the Admiralty, the Aduocatiſticall and the Procurators generall, and all other Officers, Iudges, and Iuſtices of theſe Vnited Prouinces, and to all generall Colonies, Admiralles and Vice-admirals, Captaines, Officers and Commanders, to performe, and cauſe to be performed, this order and commandement, and to proceede and cauſe to be proceeded againſt the Offenders, without grace, fauour, diſſimulation or compoſition; becauſe we haue founde it neceſſary for the good and benefite of the ſaide vnited Prouinces. Dated in *Hage* this 19. of Iuly.

F I N I S.